BACKPACK GOURMET
Good Hot Grub You Can Make at Home, Dehydrate, and Pack for Quick, Easy, and Healthy Eating on the Trail

Linda Frederick Yaffe

STACKPOLE
BOOKS

Published by
STACKPOLE BOOKS
5067 Ritter Road
Mechanicsburg, PA 17055
www.stackpolebooks.com

Printed in the United States

First Edition

10 9 8 7 6 5 4 3 2 1

Cover photograph by www.comstock.com
Cover design by Caroline Stover

Library of Congress Cataloging-in-Publication Data
Yaffe, Linda Frederick.
    Backpack gourmet : good hot grub you can make at home, dehydrate,
and pack for quick, easy, and healthy eating on the trail / Linda Frederick
Yaffe.
        p. cm.
Includes bibliographical references and index.
    ISBN 0-8117-2634-7
    1. Outdoor cookery. 2. Food—Drying. 3. Backpacking—Equipment
and supplies. I. Title.
    TX823 .Y338 2003
    641.5'78—dc21
                                                                2002010836

BACKPACK GOURMET

In memory of my grandmother,
Sarah Louise Skillman Maps, 1868–1966.
Her creativity was limitless.

. . . what does he care if he hasn't got any money: he doesn't need any money, all he needs is his rucksack with those little plastic bags of dried food and a good pair of shoes and off he goes and enjoys the privileges of a millionaire in surroundings like this.

—Jack Kerouac, *The Dharma Bums*, 1958

CONTENTS

INTRODUCTION

Homemade Lasagna at 10,000 Feet: Pack to Plate in Three Minutes

You've stopped to make camp after a long day of bushwhacking cross-country in rugged terrain. Rain clouds are moving in. You are hungry, really hungry. You want hot food *now*. Using this book, you can have it: home-cooked, ready to heat and enjoy, one-pot hot meals that you've prepared and dehydrated at home at your leisure during the past year. You pour a packet of homemade Lazy Lasagna into your pot, cover it with water, boil, stir, and enjoy.

The thrilling sport of backpacking is more popular than ever. Backpacking is our passion, but eating well in the wilderness has long been a dilemma. Universally, backpackers need generous portions of good-tasting, nutritious food—fuel that gets you over the pass—and variety to make mealtimes fun and interesting. Weight and volume are equally important: keep the pack light, with plenty of compact food inside.

Commercially freeze-dried meals are light and compact but are often flavorless, expensive, and lacking in stick-to-the-ribs satisfaction, in part because the portions are too small. All of the one-pot recipes in this book make large rehydrated portions: eighteen to twenty ounces per serving. These meals are nearly double the size of most commercial portions, which average only ten ounces per serving when rehydrated. Perhaps you have bought commercially dried food and read the small print on the label that says, "simmer for ten minutes"; this translates to twenty minutes or even longer at high altitude.

Impossibly heavy canned and fresh ingredients packed into the wilderness are not only a backbreaking burden, but are also time-consuming to prepare. Perishable foods—such as uncooked eggs, meat, or tofu—kept at the wrong temperature can make campers very ill. Containers of oil, honey, soy sauce, or other condiments in the backpack are a heavy, messy nuisance. While cooking at home is fun—with modern appliances and hot water gushing freely from the tap—in the field, an exhausted camper craves easy-to-prepare meals: no mixing, measuring, chopping, sautéing, pre-soaking, or simmering.

Perhaps you have tried drying fruits and vegetables at home to cook in camp. Drying ingredients separately and then combining them in the field is tedious and does not yield results as successful as drying complete meals—protein, grain, and sauce—all at once. When these ingredients are dried individually, they need to be soaked, sometimes for hours, before they can be incorporated into a hot meal. Dried peas, for example, can be as hard as pebbles. However, if you use the following recipes—which contain the right balance of grains, vegetables, protein, and sauce—you will discover that flavorful, nutritious one-pot dried meals can heat *fast* with no pre-soaking and no work in camp.

If you reject boring, expensive meals, or time-consuming, heavy-weight cook-in-the-field meals, you do have another choice: dry your own. Since you are simply heating—not cooking—your home-dried meals in camp, you will use far less fuel: your pack will weigh less. With a lighter pack, and larger portions of instantly prepared, better-tasting food, your backpacking adventures will soar.

CHAPTER ONE

HOME-DRIED ONE-POT MEALS

The ancient art of food dehydration is wonderfully basic. Heat and air circulation remove most of the water content from the food. This lack of water keeps microorganisms from living and growing. After many years of home-drying complete backpack meals, I have never lost food to spoilage. Follow the simple instructions in this chapter and the recipes in chapters two through five of this book and you will enjoy the same success. Dehydration is especially suited to backpacking. Not only does drying forestall spoilage, it transforms bulky, heavy food into compact, featherweight meals.

Dehydration costs less than any other method of food preservation. It requires no chemicals. Complete meals can be dried year-round in any weather, at your convenience. Take advantage of each season's bounty, using the finest fresh ingredients available, or use good-quality canned or frozen meat, fish, fruit, or vegetables. Home-dried meals can be stored for several years. It's easy to keep a ready supply of home-dried dinners on hand for carefully planned extended treks, as well as last-minute weekend escapes.

Creating home-dried one-pot meals is this simple.

Creating home-dried one-pot meals is this simple: Cook your dinner at home, slicing, grating, or dicing the ingredients into small pieces. Spread the cooked meal on covered dehydrator trays and dry until the food looks and feels completely dry. In the field, cover the food with water, boil, stir, and serve with pleasure.

Food Choices

You don't have to settle for someone else's idea of a good hot dinner. When you make your own convenience meals, you are in control: more salt or less salt, high fat or low fat, meat or meatless—the decision is yours. You can use your choice of dairy, soy, or rice milk or cheese in any of these recipes. Like it hot? Add more jalapeños. Can't eat sugar? Use a substitute. Liberate yourself from one-size-fits-all commercial meals. You enjoy good meals at home; while backpacking, you need those same good-tasting, varied, nutritionally balanced meals more than ever. Some backpackers shortchange themselves. They eat the same tired instant mashed potatoes or ramen noodles day after day. Varied, nutritionally balanced meals not only give you energy on the trail, but also keep your mind focused and make you feel happy and satisfied.

In the Home

Food Dehydrator

A high-quality electric food dehydrator with fan, heat source, and thermostat is the best food investment a backpacker can make. If you do not own a dehydrator, borrow one from a friend or relative. Try some of the recipes in this book. You will learn how simple it is to create your own one-pot meals. The dehydrator, not you, does the work.

A top-of-the-line dehydrator will pay for itself, compared to the price of commercially dried meals, during a one-week trip for a family of four. Air circulation is more important than heat when you are drying food, so be sure to choose a dehydrator with a fan as well as a heat source and a thermostat. Bargain dehydrators that lack a fan simply don't work. They will steam—not dry—your food. Either of the following brands of electric food dehydrators are recommended for decades of carefree home drying: Excalibur Products (6083 Power Inn

Road, Sacramento, CA 95824, (800) 875-4254) or Nesco American Harvest (4064 Peavey Road, Chaska, MN 55318, (800) 288-4545).

Home Kitchen Basics

All of the one-pot dehydrated meals in this book serve four hungry backpackers—two cups or more per serving when rehydrated. The four large portions indicated in these recipes will fit comfortably in typical home food dehydrators without crowding. To cook these big, full-sized backpacking portions of food, you will need to use large cooking pots at home. Here are some suggested home kitchen basics:

> Dutch oven, at least three-quart capacity
> Large ovenproof skillet, at least $10^{1}/_{2}$-inch diameter
> Soup and pasta pot, at least five-quart capacity
> Colander to drain pasta, fruits, and vegetables
> Casserole dish, at least four-quart capacity, ten by
>   thirteen inches
> Baking sheets, both flat and rimmed
> Blender or food processor to speed chopping
> Wire whisk for effortless lump-free sauces

Drying One-Pot Meals in a Dehydrator

Time-saving tip: Prepare extra food, enjoy some for dinner tonight, and dehydrate the rest.

Choose a one-pot complete meal recipe from this book. Cook your meal at home, just as though you are preparing tonight's dinner. If you choose a meal such as spaghetti, simply prepare a spaghetti sauce—your choice of beef, seafood, or vegetarian. Then boil the pasta al dente (cooked but still firm). Toss together the sauce and the drained pasta, and put the whole dish, freshly cooked and still warm, into the dehydrator. While preparing the food, chop, grate, dice, or slice the ingredients into *small pieces*. These will dehydrate much faster and more successfully than large pieces of food.

Virtually all *cooked* foods are safe and easy to dry at home. Two *uncooked* foods that should never be dried at home are eggs and milk. When cooked, these foods dehydrate safely. Many of the recipes in this book contain cooked eggs and milk. To avoid the risk of salmonella contamination, buy commercially dried powdered eggs. They are readily

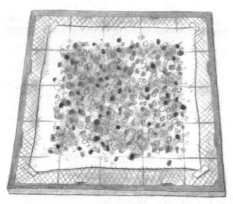

Cover mesh dehydrator trays.

available everywhere as whole eggs, egg whites, or egg substitutes for home cooking, baking, or emergencies. Dry milk is also readily available commercially as instant or regular, high or low fat, or buttermilk.

While the food is cooking, cover your mesh dehydrator trays with plastic wrap or ovenproof parchment paper. If you use plastic wrap, buy a brand made from 100 percent polyethylene. Leave about an inch of space between the wrap or paper and the edge of the trays; this will allow more air circulation. To keep the covering from shifting, you can anchor the corners with tape. If your dehydrator has solid fruit leather trays or tray covers, you do not need to use any other covering. The wrap, paper, solid trays, or tray covers simply keep liquid foods such as soups, stews, or casseroles from leaking through the mesh of the dehydrator trays.

Preheat the dehydrator for ten minutes.

Spread the warm, cooked meal evenly in a thin layer on the dehydrator trays and put them in the dehydrator. Overloaded trays dry slowly. All of the one-pot recipes in this book—which make four servings each—fit comfortably into a typical home dehydrator. For highest quality and food safety, speedy drying is best.

The meal will be completely dry in four to six hours. While your meal is drying, check it several times. To check the food and speed its drying, first wash your hands and dry them. Then pull out one tray at a time and turn and crumble the food on the tray, breaking up large pieces of food with your hands. This will ensure fast, even drying. If you are unable to check and turn the food during the drying process, a good dehydrator will successfully dry your meal anyway; drying will simply take a few hours longer. It is nearly impossible to overdry or otherwise ruin your home-dried meals using an electric dehydrator with a heat source and fan. If necessary, you can put the food in the dehydrator, leave the house, go to work for eight hours, and then turn off the dehydrator when you get home.

The recipes in this book contain some fat; backpackers need fat for fuel. However, too much fat will retard drying and could decrease the shelf life of your dried meal. While preparing your meals, carefully trim the fat from meats. Avoid excessive amounts of high-fat cheese, oil, or butter. Some especially fatty foods, such as bacon, can appear greasy during the drying process. If fat glistens on the food, simply blot it with paper towels, then return the trays to the dehydrator.

Drying times indicated in each recipe will vary due to your dehydrator and the fat and moisture content of your ingredients. The food is dry when it looks and feels dry. To test for dryness, choose a large piece of food from the dehydrator tray. Examine it and crumble it in your hand. If you notice any moisture, return the trays to the dehydrator and dry the food a bit longer. Don't worry about overdrying these meals; they are nearly foolproof.

When beans are fully dry, they feel hard and dry and can crumble into powder when crushed in your hand. Strands of spaghetti will feel dry but still slightly pliable. Meats should feel hard and leathery. Vegetables will feel hard and crisp. Fruit should be bendable and dry with no moist spots.

When the food looks and feels dry, turn off and unplug the dehydrator. Let the food rest in the dehydrator for several hours or overnight. This will let your food completely cool and release the last bits of moisture. The next day, your meal is ready to store.

Drying One-Pot Meals in an Oven

If you use an electric oven, remove the top heating element or place an empty baking sheet on the oven's top shelf. Whether your oven is electric or gas, use the *coolest* part of the oven.

To successfully dehydrate food in an oven, you need to keep the temperature low. Turn your oven to its lowest setting, usually 140 to 150 degrees Fahrenheit. Notoriously inaccurate home ovens often run 25 to 50 degrees hotter than the oven's temperature dial indicates. An oven thermometer is helpful; set it next to the drying food to keep the temperature within the 140 to 150 degree range. If the temperature rises above 150 degrees, turn off the oven for a while.

The accurate and stable Taylor Classic Oven Guide Thermometer, model 5921, can be obtained from KitchenEtc. (32 Industrial Drive, Exeter, NH 03833, (800) 232-4070, www.kitchenetc.com).

Air circulation is essential. Prop open the oven door a few inches while the food is drying. For increased air circulation, place an electric fan just outside the oven door; aim the airflow over the food.

Spread your one-pot meals in a thin layer on oiled, rimmed baking sheets. Check, shift, and crumble the food frequently while it is drying. The food around the edges of the baking sheets will dry much faster than the food in the center; protect it from scorching by checking it often.

As with an electric dehydrator, oven-dried food is dry when it looks and feels dry and crisp. Let the food cool completely for several hours or overnight before storing it.

Storing Home-Dried Meals

Bag each meal in small, sturdy plastic bags. Bag the meals according to your backpack needs. If you have dried four servings and will be backpacking in a party of two people, split the meals and store two servings per bag. If a dried meal remains high in volume after dehydration, compact it. Crush the dried meal with your hands as you pour it into the storage bag. Squeeze as much air as possible from the bag, then seal it. Double-bag the meal in a second bag; in between the two bags, place a tiny label made from a small scrap of paper with the name of the recipe, the date it was dried, how many people it will serve, and directions for rehydrating the meal. This label will tell all members of your party what the bag contains and how to prepare the meal in the field.

For best quality, store your meals in individual meal-sized bags. Avoid packing many servings of food into a single large bag that must be opened repeatedly during a long trek. Each time you open the bag, you will expose the food to air and moisture, increasing the chance of spoilage.

Store the meals in a cool, dark, dry place. Protect them from exposure to air, light, and moisture by putting the individually bagged meals into a large black plastic bag. The black bag can then be stored in a cool, dark, dry room, but, for best quality, store the meals in your refrigerator for up to two years, or in your freezer for three years. They take up little space and will be fresh and handy to throw into your pack for an unexpected weekend trip.

When you're ready to backpack, store the meals bagged in black plastic in the cool, dark, dry interior of your pack. Home-dried one-pot meals make perfect cached food for long-distance treks, since their shelf life is long.

Recycling Dehydrating Materials

The plastic wrap, ovenproof parchment paper, and all plastic food bags can be washed, dried, and reused many times before you recycle them. After each use, wash them in warm, soapy water; then rinse and dry them well.

Menu Plan

If you have ever run out of food while backpacking, forgotten a crucial item (where's the coffee?), or conversely, grumbled as you packed out five pounds of unneeded food, a menu plan will make your trip smoother. Take a few minutes to write a menu plan before you leave home. A successful trip means walking out of the wilderness carrying no food except your small emergency supply.

While planning your trip at home, draw a grid menu plan, showing three meals plus two snacks per day, and an extra snack per day for very cold weather camping. Include all of your foods and beverages, plus one extra emergency dinner and snack for each member of the party. Writing a menu plan gives you an overview of your trip. You can plan for variety: beans one night, chicken the next. Plan a soothing cheese and noodle dish the night after a jazzy, spicy dish. Serve a hot breakfast in between days of cold cereal. At the bottom of your menu grid, list the total number of servings of multiple items, such as total servings of granola, coffee, tea, cocoa, cheese, crackers, dried fruit, energy bars, and lemonade mix.

Packing the Food

Measure all servings of food. Never guess how much you will need. Using your menu plan as a guide, sit down at a table with plenty of small plastic bags and measuring cups and spoons. Carefully measure each portion into the bags. If you are backpacking for ten days or fewer, you may want to label each meal—breakfast #1, lunch #1, and dinner #1—with large-print, easy-to-read slips of paper. After you have labeled the individual meals in small bags, place them into four large plastic bags labeled breakfast, lunch, dinner, and snacks. If you are traveling in bear country and will need to hang (counterbalance) your food from a tree, take along fifty feet of nylon cord and two large nylon bags with drawstrings that can be counterbalanced from a tree limb.

To pack fragile foods, such as crackers or cookies, use waxed milk cartons or cardboard oatmeal boxes. Keep a supply of clean quart and half-gallon cartons on hand. Wash and dry the waxed cartons. Pack individual servings of fragile foods in plastic bags; then pack them tightly into the cartons. Label the cartons, and bag them in larger plastic bags. When the cartons are empty, they can be flattened and used as insulated seating during the rest of your trip while you are packing them out.

In the Field

Food Storage on the Trail

When loading your backpack each morning of your trip, put that day's snacks in an easy-to-reach outside pack pocket. Store that day's lunch near the top of the pack for easy midday access. Stow all of the rest of your food deep in the cool, dark interior of your pack.

Arriving at a possible campsite, take a few minutes to examine the area before you unpack. Choose a sleeping area; then choose a safe, protected cooking area that is at least 100 feet from your sleeping area, preferably downwind. Pick a third area for dining that is 100 feet away from your cooking and sleeping areas. Find a fourth area well away from the other three for food storage. When you travel in bear country, you will be glad you are carrying home-dried one-pot meals; since they are not cooked in the field, but merely heated, they create little odor. Nothing attracts a bear more than odiferous fresh foods such as bacon cooking on an open fire. Eliminating cooking and open fires makes your campsite far less noticeable to wild creatures.

Keep your camp spotless. Never leave food or garbage unattended unless it is properly stored. The most secure method of storage is portable bearproof aluminum containers, available for sale or rent from camping stores and national parks. Some popular backcountry camp-sites are equipped with stationary bearproof lockers. Before you pack in, check with the rangers about the availability of lockers and ask about recent bear problems. Violation of food storage regulations can result in huge fines, injury to campers, and might cause a troublesome bear to be destroyed.

In bear country, you will find trees. These trees can be used to counterbalance your food. Find a lone tree limb that is seventeen to twenty feet off the ground. It must be healthy and strong enough to support your bags of food but not thick enough to hold a young bear. Divide all of your food and all other odiferous items (toothpaste, soap, scented lotions, garbage) into two sturdy nylon bags of roughly equal weight. Tie a rock to the end of a fifty-foot length of nylon cord. Throw the rock over your chosen tree limb, then remove the rock and tie the first food bag to the end of the cord. Pull the first bag all the way up to the limb. Tie the second bag to the cord, as high as you can reach. Tie a big loop or two of cord hanging from the second bag. Use the entire cord so no end is dangling. Using a long downed branch or your walk-ing stick, push the second bag up so that the two bags are hanging side by side. The bags should hang twelve to fifteen feet above the ground. When you are ready to retrieve the bags, hook the loop of cord with your stick and gently pull the bags down.

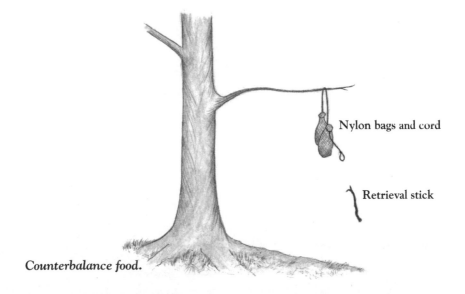

Nylon bags and cord

Retrieval stick

Counterbalance food.

When camped at the edge of or above the treeline, where trees are stunted and signs of bears are nil, cache your food well away from your tent, cooking, and dining areas. Bag your backpack in a large plastic bag and cache it a few feet off the ground on a boulder. Weight the pack with rocks. This may keep bears from seeing or smelling the food. Whichever food storage method you choose, keep your food well away from your sleeping area.

Rehydrating One-Pot Meals

These meals are ready to eat fast. Have your stove set up and ready to light. Keep a container of treated water handy. Have your pot and lid, spoons, serving cups, and home-dried meal ready. It's time for dinner.

Pour the home-dried meal into the pot. Cover the food with treated water. No measuring is necessary; simply cover soups or stews

Cover pasta, quiches, or casseroles with water just above the level of food in pot.

Cover soups or stews with water one to two inches above level of food in pot.

with plenty of water (one to two inches above the surface of the dried food in the pot), and more solid dishes such as pasta, quiches, or casseroles with barely enough water to cover (just above the surface of the dried food in the pot). Put the lid on the pot.

Light your stove. Place the pot of food on the stove. After a minute, check and stir the food. When it begins to bubble, stir until the food is fully boiling and the ingredients have softened. Turn off the stove and remove the pot. Serve and enjoy your meal.

If, while heating your meal, you find you have used too little water, simply add a bit more treated water and bring it to a full boil. If you have used a little too much water, enjoy the extra broth, or simply boil the meal a few minutes longer to reduce the extra water.

Cleanup

You've scrubbed your last sticky camping pot. When you use the recipes in this book, you will find that home-dried one-pot meals don't stick to the pot because they are not cooked in the field, but simply heated. The only cleanup equipment you will need is a drop of biodegradable soap, a minimum amount of water, and a small, weightless piece of medium-mesh nylon net (available at any fabric store) to swish away the few remaining food particles.

Using a clean container, scoop water from the deepest, cleanest nearby water source. Carry the container of water, the cooking pot, your soap, and the nylon net to a spot at least 200 feet from the water source, your camp, and any trails. Swish out the pot with a small amount of water and a drop of soap, then rinse it thoroughly. Shake the nylon net vigorously to remove water and food particles before storing it.

Field Equipment

Most people take into the woods too many utensils and of too heavy material.
—Stewart Edward White, *Camp and Trail*, 1906

The one-pot home-dried meal method requires little field equipment. Leave your frying pan, knives, forks, cutting board, plates, and extra pots at home. This is all you need:

One lightweight aluminum pot with lid (minimum size of one quart for one person, 1¹/₂ quarts for two people, two quarts for three people, three quarts for four people)

One portable stove
One windscreen
One (or more) container(s) of fuel
One lighter or large supply of matches, including water-
    and windproof
One lightweight aluminum or Lexan cup and teaspoon
    per person
One eight-inch square of regular mesh nylon net (to
    swish clean your pot and cups)
One tiny container of biodegradable liquid soap

Portable Stoves

*I took the loaf of bread, some slices of bacon, and the coffee pot
ashore, set them down by a tree, lit a fire, and went back to the
boat to get the frying-pan. While I was at this, I heard a shout
from Johnny, and looking up I saw that my fire was galloping all
over the premises!*

—Mark Twain, *Roughing It*, 1871

Like Mark Twain camping at Lake Tahoe in the nineteenth century,
many of us used to make big, smoky campfires the centerpiece of our
wilderness campsites. Much time and energy was devoted to gathering
wood, arranging kindling, and lighting and maintaining the fire while
we prepared elaborate meals, such as boiled dried beans, which took
long tedious hours to cook.

Today, wood fires seem out of place. They are illegal in many
wilderness situations, especially at the higher elevations where many
of us backpack. Wood fires damage the wilderness by (at best) scar-
ring rocks and stripping the landscape of wood, and (at worst) start-
ing wildfires—like Mark Twain's—that can destroy thousands of
acres of forest. Wood fires pollute the air and make campers and all
of their equipment reek of smoke. They attract unwelcome wildlife,
such as marauding people-wise bears, and frighten the wildlife you'd
like to see.

In an emergency, a campfire can be a necessity to warm and dry
both people and gear. Learn how to build and maintain a small, safe, hot
fire for these emergencies. Always carry wind- and waterproof matches.

The campsite without a wood fire is a cleaner, quieter place. The
peace is welcome. The darkness is friendly. One's attention is focused
upon the stars, the trees, and the wind, rather than the campfire.

Today's superb selection of clean, hot, and easy-to-operate portable stoves for backpackers and paddlers provides many good choices. Consider which features best suit your most frequent style of wilderness travel.

Liquid Fuel Stoves

Liquid fuel stoves burn white gas (in North America), kerosene (everywhere else in the world), auto gas, or diesel.

Advantages: They provide a hot flame. The fuel bottle is refillable. There is no canister to discard. You can carry just as much fuel as you need for the length of your trip. They are reliable, can be repaired in the field, and inexpensive fuel can be obtained nearly anywhere.

Disadvantages: Liquid fuel stoves burn hot, which means quickly boiled water and quickly rehydrated home-dried meals, but this fuel can burn quite hot for the kind of traditional cooking that requires simmering. These stoves need pumping and priming to pressurize and light; they require a bit of practice and caution to prevent flare-ups.

Canister Stoves

Canisters are filled with fuels, or a blend of fuels, such as propane, butane, isobutane, or isopropane.

Advantages: Canister stoves are very clean. They are extremely easy and safe to operate. Flare-ups are not a problem. You simply turn on the stove and light it.

Disadvantages: These pressurized canisters are not refillable. Since they can only be used once, the empty canisters must be packed out and discarded (most cannot be recycled). Canisters are not as readily available as liquid fuel, and canisters are more expensive. These stoves

Liquid fuel stove

do not burn hot enough to work well in cold temperatures or high winds, or when the fuel is low. In addition, it is hard to judge how much fuel is left in the canister.

Portable Stove Overview

If you backpack in warm summer conditions with youngsters in your party, a canister stove is wonderfully safe and easy. If you take long trips, travel internationally with a backpack, and/or backpack in below-freezing weather, a liquid fuel stove is a good choice. All portable stoves are perfect for quickly heating your home-dried one-pot meals.

Time- and money-saving tip: Your home-dried one-pot meals are just as convenient for car camping and traveling as they are for backpacking. When traveling at home or abroad, use a portable one-burner electric "buffet" stove to easily prepare the meals in your room. Be sure to carry a portable electrical converter when traveling away from the Americas to modify the voltage. Never use an outdoor stove indoors.

Safe Water

> I stop to drink. The water is bitterly, brilliantly cold, with particles of glacial grit—utterly delicious.
> —Edward Abbey, Desert Solitaire, 1968

The water rushing over rocks, shooting bubbly plumes into the air, forming blue pools, looks so clean, so inviting. Can you safely dip your cup into the clear blue pool and enjoy a refreshing drink?

Today, pollution from larger numbers of careless outdoorspeople and infected wildlife compel you to treat all of the water you drink, use to clean your teeth, and use to prepare your food. Never drink untreated water, no matter how "clean" it appears. Most of the surface water in the United States is contaminated with Giardia lamblia and Cryptosporidium. These disease-causing microorganisms are invisible to the naked eye. They can make you seriously ill, causing months of stomach cramps, diarrhea, nausea, dehydration, and fatigue. Cases of Giardia, the most common waterborne pathogen, have more than doubled in the United States during the past decade.

Giardia and Cryptosporidium are spread through fecal-oral transmission. They are passed from person to person and from domestic and wild animals to humans. You can avoid spreading these pathogens by using good field practices and common sense. Camp at least 200 feet from any water source. Properly bury your feces, pack out toilet paper, and always wash your hands thoroughly with soap and water after defecating or changing a diaper and before handling food. When scouting for a water source, use the best-looking one available. Avoid water that contains floating material or water with a dark color or an odor. Filter murky water through a clean cloth before treating it.

Fortunately, you can choose from several effective drinking water treatment methods: boiling, filtering, purifying, ultraviolet purification, or chemical treatment (tablets). Choose the method or combination of methods that suit the locale of your trip, your style of camping for the trip, and your personal preference.

Treated Water from Home

Carry plenty of treated water from home. Always carry five to ten gallons of treated water from home in your vehicle. Pack in as much as you can comfortably carry and have plenty available in your vehicle when you pack out of the wilderness.

Boiling

This is the most effective, fail-safe field treatment method. Vigorously boil untreated water for one to two minutes to kill the microorganisms that can make you ill.

Advantages: This is a very effective and inexpensive method. Anyone with a cooking pot, a stove and fuel, or the resources to build an open fire, can treat as much water as they need, anywhere in the world.

Disadvantages: Boiling all of your drinking water is inconvenient unless you are staying in a base camp. It is time and fuel consuming to boil quantities of water, and then let it cool enough to drink. While you are base-camped, it is feasible to spend the evenings boiling and filling containers with purified water, but it is a big chore. Boiled water, having lost oxygen in the process, tastes unpleasantly flat. Aeration (pouring the boiled water back and forth from one clean container to another) can improve the flat taste. Try letting the boiled water stand for several hours or overnight, or add a small pinch of salt to each quart of boiled water to improve the flavor. Since the taste of good mountain water is one of the attractions of a wilderness adventure, boiled water makes the trip less special.

Water Filters

Choose a modern microporous water filter to pump water from a groundwater source into your water container. Look for a filter that has an absolute pore size of one micron or less for protection from Cryptosporidium as well as *Giardia*.

Advantages: Cool, good-tasting treated water is available immediately. In areas of frequent surface water availability, the filter weighs far less than extra containers filled with clean water.

Disadvantages: Filters weigh from eleven to twenty-three ounces. They are costly. You need to clean filters regularly and periodically replace the filtering cartridges. Filters do not protect against waterborne viruses such as polio and hepatitis. Waterborne viruses are rare in North America but prevalent in some other parts of the world.

Water Purifiers

These are water filters with an added purifying device that forces the water through chlorine beads, killing most viruses as well as the *Giardia* and Cryptosporidium parasites.

Advantages: Worry-free water treatment.

Disadvantages: Purifiers are slightly heavier and more costly than regular water filters.

Ultraviolet Purification

A portable battery-powered wand uses ultraviolet light to neutralize bacteria, viruses, and protozoa.

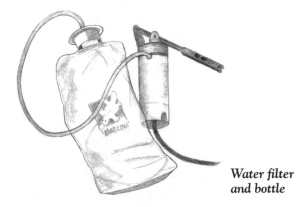

*Water filter
and bottle*

Advantages: The wand is fast and easy to use: Just swish the device around in a container of water. No pumping is required, and there are no chemical flavors.

Disadvantages: This technology is new to the backcountry. It is costly.

Water Purification Tablets

Tiny, lightweight tablets kill viruses in groundwater, but they do not effectively eliminate *Giardia* or Cryptosporidium.

Advantages: Convenient and lightweight, the tablets effectively kill waterborne viruses. They can be used as emergency substitutes only when you are unable to boil or filter your water. Potable Aqua treatment tablets, used with P.A. Plus, which is added twenty minutes after the first tablets, erase the unpleasant iodine taste of the initial tablets. The flavor can be further improved by letting the water stand for several hours or by adding powdered drink mix.

Disadvantages: Not as effective as boiling, filtering, purifying, or ultraviolet purification, tablets are an excellent supplement to filtering your water in parts of the world where viruses are a threat.

CHAPTER TWO

BREAKFAST AND LUNCH

Breakfast

Hot or cold, choose trailside breakfasts that are filling, nutritious, and easy to prepare, so you can start your day without fuss. Breakfast bars are the ultimate in fast meals. Granola is truly instant if you've premeasured servings at home that include dry milk and chopped fruit; just add a dash of water from your bottle and you're ready to enjoy an energy-packed breakfast. Complete hot meals such as Breakfast Grits, Bacon, and Eggs can be ready, pack to plate, in three minutes—the time it takes to boil water—if you've dried your own one-pot meals at home, at your leisure.

Hot Beverages

Camper's Coffee
Weight 1 serving = fraction of an ounce

Here's an easy, lightweight camp coffee-making solution. At home, bag instant coffee crystals in a plastic bag, allowing one heaping teaspoon per cup. Take extra—instant coffee is nearly weightless. In camp, boil one cup of water per serving. While the water is boiling, stir one heaping teaspoon of instant coffee per cup into the pot. Cover the pot, turn off the stove, and let the coffee rest for thirty seconds. Pour and enjoy coffee that tastes freshly brewed.

Trail Tea
Weight 1 serving = fraction of an ounce

Loose tea leaves taste best and are the best backpacking choice. Tea bag paper doesn't decompose and must be packed out. At home, bag loose tea leaves (black or green tea leaves or herbal substitutes) one scant teaspoon per cup. Take extra—tea leaves are nearly weightless. In camp, boil one cup of water per serving. Turn off the stove and stir in one scant teaspoon of tea leaves per cup. Cover the pot and let the tea steep for three minutes or more, to your taste. Strain the tea through a fine-mesh nylon net into your cup. Disperse the tea leaves away from your camp, and shake the remaining tea leaves off the nylon net before storing it.

Instant Cocoa

Weight 1 serving = 1 ounce

For each serving: At home, mix together in a small plastic bag:

3 teaspoons instant dry milk
2 teaspoons packed brown sugar
1 1/2 teaspoons unsweetened cocoa powder

In camp, pour a bag of instant cocoa mix into a cup. Add while stirring well:

1 cup boiling water

Café Mocha

Weight 1 serving = 1.5 ounces

For each serving: At home, mix together in a small plastic bag:

1 tablespoon packed brown sugar
1 tablespoon instant dry milk
1 teaspoon unsweetened cocoa powder
1 teaspoon instant coffee crystals

In camp, pour a bag of mocha mix into a cup. Add while stirring well:

1 cup boiling water

Commercially available hot cider mix provides variety at breakfast time or in the evening.

Hot Breakfast Combinations

Celebration Brunch

Serves 4
Weight 1 dried serving = 6 ounces

This dish will make any morning a celebration.

1. Bring to a boil in a large saucepan:

   9 medium baking potatoes (about 3¹/2 pounds), peeled
   8 cups water

   Simmer for 30 minutes, or until fork-tender. Drain the potatoes, then use a potato masher or fork to mash them in the pot, along with:

   2 tablespoons butter or margarine
   1¹/2 pounds tofu
   1 teaspoon salt
   ¹/4 teaspoon ground nutmeg

   Set aside.

2. Meanwhile, heat a large skillet over medium-low heat. Add:

   2 tablespoons olive oil

   When the oil is hot, add:

   2 onions, minced
   4 cloves garlic, minced

   Cook for 8 minutes, then add, stirring occasionally, until just set:

   8 eggs, beaten
   2 tablespoons chopped fresh basil or parsley leaves
   1 teaspoon salt
   ¹/2 teaspoon ground white pepper
   ¹/2 teaspoon crushed red pepper flakes

3. Preheat oven to 350 degrees. Oil a 10-by-13-inch casserole dish.

4. Spread the potato mixture in the casserole dish. Sprinkle with:

   1 cup finely grated Parmesan cheese

   Spread the egg mixture evenly over the top of the casserole. Bake for 10 minutes.

5. Using a spatula, mix the casserole and spread on covered dehydrator trays.

6. Dehydrate for 6 hours at 145 degrees.

7. To rehydrate, cover with water just above level of food in pot, boil, stir, and serve.

Breakfast Casserole
Serves 4
Weight 1 dried serving = 5.5 ounces

1. Heat a skillet over medium-low heat. Add:
   1 tablespoon olive oil
   When the oil is hot, add:
   1 onion, minced
   10 fresh mushrooms, minced
   Cook for 7 minutes, stirring occasionally.
2. Preheat oven to 325 degrees. Oil a 10-by-13-inch casserole dish. Place in the dish:
   8^{1}/2 cups day-old whole-grain bread cubes
   Sprinkle over the bread cubes:
   2 cups grated cheddar cheese
   Spoon the mushroom mixture over the cheese.
3. Beat together in a large bowl:
   9 eggs
   2^{1}/2 cups milk
   ^{1}/4 cup minced fresh parsley leaves
   1 teaspoon salt
   ^{1}/2 teaspoon cayenne pepper
4. Pour the egg mixture over the bread, cheese, and mushrooms.
5. Bake for 20 minutes, or until firm.
6. Spread on covered dehydrator trays and dehydrate for 5^{1}/2 hours at 145 degrees.
7. To rehydrate, cover with water just above level of food in pot, boil, stir, and serve.

French Country Potatoes
Serves 4
Weight 1 dried serving = 6.5 ounces

In rural France, potatoes are not whipped but gently crushed with plenty of garlic.

1. Cover with water and boil for 25 minutes, or until fork-tender:
   9 whole medium baking potatoes (about 4^{1}/2 pounds),
   scrubbed but not peeled.
   Drain the potatoes. Let them cool slightly; then peel them and return them to the pot. Mash the potatoes coarsely with a fork.

2. Heat a Dutch oven over medium-low heat: Add:
>   **3 tablespoons olive oil**

When the oil is hot, add:
>   **2 onions, minced**

Sauté for 5 minutes, or until light brown. Reduce heat; add the potatoes and:
>   **2 tablespoons butter or margarine**
>   **1¹/₂ pounds tofu, crumbled**
>   **8 cloves garlic, minced**
>   **1 teaspoon salt**
>   **¹/₂ teaspoon freshly ground black pepper**
>   **¹/₄ teaspoon ground nutmeg**

Cook for 10 minutes, stirring occasionally.

3. Remove from heat and stir in:
>   **1³/₄ cups crumbled chèvre (goat cheese)**

4. Spread on covered dehydrator trays and dehydrate for 6 hours at 145 degrees.

5. To rehydrate, cover with water just above level of food in pot, boil, stir, and serve.

Packer's Potatoes Plus

Serves 4
Weight 1 dried serving = 6 ounces

These potatoes pack a protein punch.

1. Preheat oven to 425 degrees.

2. Place on a baking sheet:
>   **7 medium baking potatoes (about 3¹/₂ pounds), scrubbed but not peeled, pricked with a fork**

3. Bake the potatoes for 40 minutes, or until fork-tender. Let the potatoes cool slightly; then dice them.

4. Heat a Dutch oven over medium-low heat. Add:
>   **1 tablespoon olive oil**

When the oil is hot, add and cook for 4 minutes:
>   **1 onion, minced**

Add the diced potatoes and:
>   **3 cloves garlic, minced**

Cook for 6 minutes, stirring occasionally.

5. Reduce heat and stir in:
     3 1/2 **cups spaghetti sauce**
     1/2 **cup salsa, mild, medium, or hot**
     15 **ounces canned pinto beans, rinsed and drained**
     1/2 **teaspoon salt**
   Mix all ingredients well.
6. Spread on covered dehydrator trays and dehydrate for 6 hours at 145 degrees.
7. To rehydrate, cover with water 1 1/2 inches above level of food in pot, boil, stir, and serve.

Baked Breakfast Pasta

Serves 4
Weight 1 dried serving = 5.5 ounces

This is an easy egg and pasta dish.
1. Cook, then drain in a colander:
     12 **ounces vermicelli pasta, broken in thirds**
2. Preheat oven to 350 degrees. Oil a 10-by-13-inch casserole dish.
3. Beat together in the pasta pot:
     6 **eggs, beaten**
     3 1/2 **cups spaghetti sauce**
     15 **ounces canned small white beans, rinsed and drained**
     3 **cloves garlic, minced**
     1/2 **cup grated mozzarella cheese**
     1/2 **cup finely grated Parmesan cheese**
     1/2 **teaspoon salt**
     1/4 **teaspoon cayenne pepper**
   Add the cooked pasta and stir well.
4. Spread the pasta in the casserole dish. Bake for 25 minutes.
5. Spread on covered dehydrator trays and dehydrate for 5 hours at 145 degrees.
6. To rehydrate, cover with water 1/2 inch above level of food in pot, boil, stir, and serve.

Hash Browns with
Eggs and Sausage

Serves 4
Weight 1 dried serving = 5 ounces

Enjoy this complete breakfast in only 3 minutes from pack to plate.

1. Grate, then drain in a colander, pressing out moisture:

   **10 medium baking potatoes (about 4^1/$_2$ pounds),
   scrubbed but not peeled**

   2 large onions

2. Heat a Dutch oven over medium heat, then add:

   2 tablespoons olive oil

   When the oil is hot, add the potatoes and onion, pressing them into the pan and stirring occasionally, for 10 minutes.

3. Stir in:

   10 ounces beef, pork, turkey, or soy sausage, minced

   1 teaspoon salt

   1 teaspoon freshly ground black pepper

   Reduce heat to very low, cover, and cook for 10 minutes, stirring occasionally.

4. Preheat oven to 350 degrees. Oil a 10-by-13-inch casserole dish.

5. Stir into the potato mixture:

   8 eggs, beaten

   ^{1}/$_2$ cup finely grated Parmesan cheese

   Spread the mixture in the casserole dish. Bake for 20 minutes, or until golden brown.

6. Spread on covered dehydrator trays and dehydrate for 4^1/$_2$ hours at 145 degrees.

7. To rehydrate, cover with water ^{1}/$_2$ inch above level of food in pot, boil, stir, and serve.

Breakfast Grits,
Bacon, and Eggs

Serves 4
Weight 1 dried serving = 7 ounces

This is spicy.

1. Heat in a heavy saucepan just until boiling:

   5 cups milk

   ^{1}/$_4$ teaspoon salt

   ^{1}/$_2$ teaspoon freshly ground black pepper

   2 tablespoons butter or margarine

2. Add slowly, stirring constantly:
   2 cups quick-cooking white grits
   6 eggs, beaten
3. Reduce heat. Stir in and cook 3 minutes longer:
   ³/4 cup pork or soy bacon bits
   1 teaspoon hot sauce
   1 cup grated sharp cheese (Swiss or Cheddar)
   ¹/2 cup finely grated Parmesan cheese
4. Spread on covered dehydrator trays and dehydrate for 5 hours at 145 degrees.
5. To rehydrate, cover with water ¹/2 inch above level of food in pot, boil, stir, and serve.

Country Quiche

Serves 4
Weight 1 dried serving = 5.5 ounces

1. Heat a Dutch oven over low heat. Add:
   2 tablespoons olive oil
 When the oil is hot, add:
   2 onions, minced
   8 fresh mushrooms, minced
   6 medium baking potatoes (about 2³/4 pounds), grated
 Cook for 15 minutes, stirring occasionally.
2. Stir in:
   ³/4 cup any variety stock, milk, or water
 Cover, reduce to very low heat, and cook 5 minutes longer.
3. Preheat oven to 350 degrees. Oil a 10-by-13-inch casserole dish.
4. Beat together in a large bowl:
   7 eggs
   2 cups milk
   1 cup TVP (textured vegetable protein—cooked, dried soybean flakes available at health food stores)
   1 cup finely grated Parmesan or Romano cheese
   ³/4 teaspoon salt
   ¹/8 teaspoon freshly ground black pepper
   ¹/8 teaspoon cayenne pepper
   ¹/8 teaspoon ground nutmeg
 Let stand for 5 minutes; then add the potato mixture and beat well.
5. Pour the mixture into the casserole dish. Bake for 25 minutes, or until a toothpick inserted in center comes out clean.

6. Spread on covered dehydrator trays and dehydrate for 6 hours at 145 degrees.
7. To rehydrate, cover with water $1/2$ inch above level of food in pot, boil, stir, and serve.

Honeymoon Lake Cheese Noodles

Serves 4
Weight 1 dried serving = 6.5 ounces

This is a slightly sweet and cheesy treat.
1. Cook, then drain in a colander:
    12 ounces vermicelli pasta, broken in thirds
2. Preheat oven to 350 degrees. Oil a 10-by-13-inch casserole dish.
3. Return the pasta to the pot and add:
    2 tablespoons butter or margarine
    1 sweet onion, minced
    $1/4$ cup minced fresh basil or parsley
    12 ounces canned evaporated milk
    1 cup plain yogurt
    1 teaspoon salt
    $1/2$ teaspoon crushed red pepper flakes
    $1/8$ teaspoon cayenne pepper
    $3/4$ cup TVP (textured vegetable protein)
    4 eggs, beaten
    $3/4$ cup grated sharp cheddar cheese
    $1/4$ cup finely grated Parmesan cheese
4. Pour the pasta mixture into the casserole dish. Sprinkle evenly over the top:
    1 cup bread or cracker crumbs
    Dot with:
    1 tablespoon butter or margarine
5. Bake for 25 minutes, or until toothpick inserted in center comes out clean.
6. Spread on covered dehydrator trays and dehydrate for 5 hours at 145 degrees.
7. To rehydrate, cover with water $1/2$ inch above level of food in pot, boil, stir, and serve.

Cheese Blintz Casserole

1. To make the crepes, heat a griddle or skillet over medium heat. Mix together in a medium bowl:
   - **1 cup whole wheat flour**
   - **1 cup unbleached white flour**
   - **1 tablespoon packed brown sugar**
   - **2 teaspoons baking powder**
2. Beat together in a small bowl:
   - **2 eggs**
   - **1 teaspoon vanilla**
   - **2¹/₂ cups milk**
3. Add the egg mixture to the flour mixture and beat briefly.
4. Lightly oil the preheated griddle or skillet. Pour 4 tablespoons of batter onto the griddle. Cook crepe until bottom is browned; then turn and cook until other side is browned. Keep crepes warm until all (twelve 6-inch-diameter crepes) are cooked.
5. Make the filling. Mix together in a large bowl:
   - **2 cups cottage cheese**
   - **3 cups plain yogurt**
   - **2 bunches scallions, minced**
   - **1¹/₄ cups finely grated Parmesan cheese**
   - **¹/₂ teaspoon ground nutmeg**
   - **¹/₄ teaspoon freshly ground black pepper**
6. Preheat oven to 350 degrees. Oil a 10-by-13-inch casserole dish.
7. Place six of the crepes evenly over the bottom of the dish. Cover with half of the filling. Repeat with a final layer of crepes and filling. Bake for 25 minutes or until bubbly.
8. Spread on covered dehydrator trays, breaking up the crepes with a spatula.
9. Dehydrate for 5 hours at 145 degrees.
10. To rehydrate, cover with water ¹/₂ inch above level of food in pot, boil, stir, and serve.

Breakfast Pudding

Serves 4
Weight 1 serving (1 cup) = 3.5 ounces

1. Toast for 5 minutes in a skillet over low heat:
   $^1/_2$ cup any variety chopped nuts
   $^1/_2$ cup shredded coconut
   Let cool slightly.
2. Combine the nuts and coconut in a plastic bag along with:
   1 cup instant dry milk
   1 cup confectioners' sugar
   6 tablespoons cornstarch
   4 tablespoons cocoa powder (optional)
   $^1/_8$ teaspoon salt
2. In camp, pour the contents of the bag into the cooking pot. Cover
   with 4 cups of treated water. Bring to a boil, stirring constantly after
   it begins to thicken. Serve warm.

Hot Cereal

Instant Oatmeal

Serves 4
Weight 1 serving = 4.5 ounces

*This is tastier, cheaper, and provides far larger portions than the commercial
variety.*
1. Grind to a powder in a blender or food processor:
   2 cups regular rolled oats
   $^1/_4$ cup any variety nuts
2. Place the powder in a plastic bag and add:
   1 cup instant dry milk
   $^1/_2$ cup packed brown sugar
   $^1/_4$ teaspoon ground cinnamon
   $^1/_4$ cup any variety chopped dried fruit
3. In camp, cover with water 3 inches above level of food in pot. Stir
   while bringing to a boil. Serve immediately.

Quick Hot Cereal

Serves 4
Weight 1 serving = 4.5 ounces

1. Mix together in a plastic bag:
   2 cups whole wheat couscous
   $^1/_4$ cup instant dry milk
   $^1/_4$ cup packed brown sugar
   $^1/_4$ cup chopped dried fruit
   $^1/_4$ cup any variety finely chopped nuts
   $^1/_8$ teaspoon salt
2. In the field, cover with water 1 inch above level of food in pot. Boil, stir, and serve.

Cold Cereal

Honey Nut Granola

18 servings
Weight 1 serving = 4 ounces

This is a satisfying, ready-to-eat breakfast.
1. Toast in a large skillet over medium heat, stirring frequently, until light brown:
   2 cups whole wheat flour
   1 cup wheat germ
   1 cup flaked coconut
   1 cup brewer's yeast (high-protein dried unleavened yeast)
2. Preheat oven to 350 degrees.
3. Heat gently in a saucepan until warm:
   $^1/_2$ cup canola oil
   1 cup honey
   1 cup packed brown sugar
   $^1/_2$ cup apple juice
4. Mix together in a 10-by-13-inch casserole dish:
   7 cups rolled oats
   $^1/_2$ cup hulled sunflower seeds
   2 cups any variety chopped nuts
5. Pour the flour and honey mixtures over the oat mixture in the casserole dish. Mix well.

6. Bake for 15 minutes, stir; then bake 15 minutes longer. Turn off the oven. Stir the granola; then let it stand in the oven with the door closed for 2 hours.
7. Cool completely; then double-bag and store in the freezer until ready to use.
8. Before camping, package individual servings of granola in 6^1/$_2$-inch-square plastic sandwich bags. Place in each bag:

^{3}/$_4$ cup granola
2 tablespoons instant dry milk
1 tablespoon any variety chopped dried fruit

To serve, pour one bag of granola mixture into a cup. Fill cup with cool treated water, stir, and enjoy.

Sweet Morning Granola

20 servings
Weight 1 serving = 4 ounces

1. Heat a large skillet over medium-low heat. Toast in the skillet, stirring frequently, for 8 minutes:

2 cups whole wheat flour
1 cup wheat germ
1 cup flaked coconut
^{1}/$_2$ cup sesame seeds

2. Preheat oven to 350 degrees.
3. Heat gently in a saucepan until warm:

1 cup peanut butter
^{1}/$_2$ cup canola oil
^{1}/$_2$ cup honey
^{3}/$_4$ cup brown sugar
1 tablespoon vanilla extract

4. Mix together in a 10-by-13-inch casserole dish:

8 cups rolled oats
1 cup any variety chopped nuts

5. Pour the browned flour and peanut butter mixtures over the oat mixture. Combine thoroughly.
6. Bake for 15 minutes, stir; then bake 10 minutes longer. Turn off the heat. Stir the granola; then let it stand in the oven with the door closed for 2 hours.
7. Cool completely; then double-bag and store in the freezer until ready to use.

8. Before camping, package individual servings of granola in 6^1/$_2$-inch-square plastic sandwich bags. Place in each bag:

   ^{3}/$_4$ cup granola
   2 tablespoons instant dry milk
   1 tablespoon any variety chopped dried fruit

   To serve, pour one bag of granola mixture into a cup. Fill cup with cool treated water, stir, and enjoy.

Muesli

12 servings
Weight 1 serving = 3.5 ounces

This Swiss-style cereal is ready-to-eat.
1. Toast in a skillet over medium heat for 3 minutes or until golden brown:

   3 cups quick rolled oats
2. Place the oats in a large bowl. Add and mix:

   3 cups sliced almonds   **2 cups flaked coconut**
   1 cup chopped dried fruit   **1 cup packed brown sugar**
   2 cups instant dry milk
3. To store, place in ^{3}/$_4$-cup portions in small plastic bags. Store in freezer or refrigerator prior to trip.
4. To serve, pour one bag of muesli into a cup. Fill the cup with cool treated water, stir, and enjoy.

Potpourri Cold Cereal

1 serving
Weight 1 serving = 3 ounces

Vary this dish by using different cereals, fruits, and nuts.
1. Mix together in a small plastic bag:

   ^{1}/$_4$ cup puffed wheat cereal
   ^{1}/$_4$ cup puffed rice cereal
   ^{1}/$_4$ cup bran flakes cereal
   2 tablespoons flaked coconut
   2 tablespoons instant dry milk
   1 tablespoon quick rolled oats
   1 tablespoon any variety chopped dried fruit
   1 tablespoon any variety chopped nuts
   1 teaspoon packed brown sugar
2. To serve, pour one bag of cereal into a cup. Fill with cool treated water, stir, and enjoy.

Breakfast Bars

Toffee-Nut Breakfast Squares

24 servings
Weight 1 serving (1 square) = 2 ounces

You don't need to bake these bars.
1. Oil a 10-by-13-inch glass casserole dish.
2. Mix together in a large bowl:
   > **8 cups puffed rice cereal**
   > **2 cups any variety nuts, chopped**
3. Gently heat in a saucepan just until bubbling:
   > **10 ounces English toffee bits**
   > **³/4 cup honey**
4. Pour the toffee mixture over the cereal mixture. Mix well, then press firmly into the casserole dish.
5. Cover and refrigerate for 2 hours or until firm. Bring to room temperature.
6. Cut into 24 squares. Wrap squares individually before storing at room temperature.

Granola Bars

8 servings
Weight 1 serving (1 bar) = 4.5 ounces

1. Toast in a skillet over low heat for 3 minutes, stirring frequently, until light brown:
   > **1 cup any variety nuts, chopped**
   > **1 cup shredded coconut**
   Set aside.
2. Mix together in a large bowl:
   > **2 cups rolled oats**
   > **1 cup whole wheat flour**
   > **1 cup graham cracker crumbs (5 whole crackers)**
   Cut in:
   > **¹/2 cup chilled butter or margarine**
   Stir in the toasted nuts and coconut and:
   > **¹/2 cup honey**
   > **¹/2 cup packed brown sugar**
3. Preheat oven to 275 degrees. Oil a 10-by-6-inch pan.

4. Pat the mixture firmly into the pan. Bake for 50 minutes or until light brown.
5. Cut into 8 bars while still warm; then let them cool completely in the pan on a wire rack.
6. Store in individual serving-sized bags.

Karen's Oatmeal Breakfast Cake
16 servings
Weight 1 serving = 4 ounces

---

1. Stir together in a large, heatproof bowl:

   1 cup rolled oats   1 cup honey
   $^1/_2$ cup canola oil $1^1/_3$ cups boiling water

   Let cool for 20 minutes.
2. Preheat oven to 350 degrees. Oil a 10-by-13-inch casserole dish.
3. Add to the oat mixture:

   2 eggs
   $^3/_4$ cup yogurt
   $^1/_2$ cup packed brown sugar
   $1^1/_2$ cups whole wheat flour
   2 tablespoons toasted wheat germ
   2 tablespoons brewer's yeast
   2 tablespoons instant dry milk
   2 teaspoons ground cinnamon
   1 teaspoon baking powder
   $^1/_2$ teaspoon baking soda
   1 cup any variety nuts, finely chopped

   Beat well.
4. Pour the batter into the prepared dish.
5. Bake for 25 minutes, or until toothpick inserted in center comes out clean.
6. Let cool completely before cutting into 16 servings. Store servings in individual bags.

Variation: Oatmeal Breakfast Slices
16 servings
Weight 1 serving = 1.5 ounces

To decrease weight and volume and increase storage life, follow the above recipe then slice each serving in half horizontally. Place the slices cut side down on ungreased baking sheets. Bake in a preheated 200 degree oven for 30 minutes; then turn the slices over and bake them 30 minutes longer. Let cool completely before storing in individual serving-sized bags. One serving (two rebaked slices) weighs only 1.5 ounces, less than half the weight of a fresh serving.

Lunch

When you've planned and completely prepared your lunches at home, you have more time for eating and relaxing during wonderful view-filled mountain lunch breaks. Consider a practical hot lunch when rain seems likely later in the day, or when you are taking your lunch break near a water source but will be making a "dry camp" with a cold picnic dinner that evening.

For quick lunches eaten directly from your pack, plan a variety of combinations of breads, proteins, and vegetables.

About Breads

Good choices of breads are crackers, flatbread (chapatis, tortillas, pita bread), zwieback, rice cakes, and tortilla chips. Make your own special backpack crackers; they are far tastier and fresher than commercial ones. Make several kinds to provide variety on long trips. Homemade crackers keep amazingly well and are extremely lightweight. Ready-to-eat commercial rice cakes and tortilla chips make a nice change. Homemade chapatis are a wonderful standby, as are commercially made flour tortillas. These flatbreads will keep for a week and are excellent filled with spreads or dips. Long-keeping breads such as pumpernickel are appropriate during shorter trips and will remain fresh for the first four or five days of longer trips.

To pack breads, store them in individual serving-sized plastic bags to preclude frequent opening of the same large bag, exposing the crackers or bread to the air. Keep them dry by placing them in several layers of plastic bags. Keep crackers and other fragile foods from being crushed; carry them in waxed cartons or oatmeal boxes (see "Packing the Food," chapter one).

About Protein Foods

Good protein choices include cheese; home-dried bean, cheese, meat or fish spreads; fish or meat jerky; dry sausage; and peanut butter. Protect all protein foods from heat and mold. Cheeses that keep well long-term in the pack include hard, dense, aged cheeses, such as Parmesan, cheddar, Romano, or dry Monterey Jack. Small wax-covered cheeses such as Edam, Gouda, and smoked cheddar are a good choice, too. Beware of soft cheeses, which require refrigeration; read the label before you buy.

Homemade jerky is easy to make. Store the jerky in your refrigerator or freezer at home prior to your trip. Keep it cool and dry in your pack while on the trail.

Read the label carefully before purchasing dry sausages; these include chorizo (spicy Spanish), pepperoni (air dried), and Genoa Salami (with wine and garlic). The label must say "keep refrigerated" if that is necessary. Look for dry sausage that does not need refrigeration, and check the label's "use by" date. Dry sausages should be purchased in small rolls, kept cool, and used quickly once sliced.

Peanut butter packs well in refillable squeeze tubes. Jelly, preserves, chutney, or mustard can easily be carried the same way. Squeeze the peanut butter directly onto crackers or bread—no spreading tool is needed.

About Raw Vegetables

Pack raw vegetables and dried vegetable dips for your trips. It's far easier to prepare your vegetables at home than on the trail. If you precut and package lunch portions of cheese and wash and precut vegetables, you don't need to pull out your knife. At home, wash and cut the vegetables you will need during the first four or five days of your backpack trip. Wrap them in a slightly damp clean bandana and bag them well in two layers of plastic bags. Never wash fruit or vegetables with untreated water on the trail. Long-keeping raw vegetables include whole baby carrots, scallions, onions, zucchini, cucumbers, and tomatoes. Medium-keeping ones include celery, bell peppers, sugar or snap peas, romaine lettuce, and watercress.

Drinks

Powdered fruit juice and sports drinks provide the liquid and sugar that you need. The following mix will help replace sodium and potassium lost during exertion.

Trail Rehydration Drink

1 serving
Weight 1 serving = 0.25 ounce

1. Mix together in a plastic bag:
    1 teaspoon powdered lemonade mix
    $^1/_{16}$ teaspoon salt
2. On the trail, pour the mix into a cup. Fill cup with cool treated water, stir, and serve.

Egg Nog

1 serving
Weight 1 serving = 1.5 ounces

Try this cool smoothie at lunchtime.
1. At home, mix together in individual serving-sized plastic bags:
    2 tablespoons instant dry milk
    1 tablespoon powdered egg whites
    1 teaspoon brown sugar
    $^1/_2$ teaspoon instant coffee crystals
    dash cinnamon
    dash nutmeg
2. To serve, pour 1 bagful into a cup. Fill with cool treated water, stir, and enjoy.

Breads

Multigrain Chapatis

4 servings
Weight 1 serving (3 chapatis) = 4 ounces

These sturdy flatbreads pack well.
1. Grind to a powder in a blender or food processor:
    2 tablespoons rolled oats

Combine the oat flour (about 2 tablespoons) in a medium bowl along with:

> 1 cup whole wheat flour
> 1 cup unbleached white flour
> $^1/_2$ teaspoon salt
> $^1/_8$ teaspoon cayenne pepper

2. Cut in:

> 2 tablespoons chilled butter or margarine

3. Stir in:

> $^3/_4$ cup warm water

Knead well to form a smooth ball. Cover and let stand for 1 hour.

4. Heat ungreased griddle or skillet over medium heat.
5. Divide the dough into 12 pieces.
6. On a floured board, roll out each piece of dough as thin as possible into rough $7^1/_2$-inch circles.
7. Bake on griddle for several minutes, turning two or three times, until very light brown.
8. Let cool completely on wire racks before double-bagging in individual serving-sized bags.

Spicy Seed Chapatis

4 servings
Weight 1 serving (3 chapatis) = 4 ounces

1. Toast in a skillet over low heat for 4 minutes, stirring frequently, until light brown:

> 1 tablespoon sesame seeds
> 1 tablespoon flax seeds

2. Combine the toasted seeds in a medium bowl along with:

> 1 cup whole wheat flour
> 1 cup unbleached white flour
> 1 teaspoon crushed red pepper flakes
> $^1/_2$ teaspoon salt

3. Cut in:

> 2 tablespoons chilled butter or margarine

4. Stir in:

> $^3/_4$ cup warm water

Knead well to form a smooth ball. Cover and let stand for 1 hour.

5. Heat ungreased griddle or skillet over medium heat.
6. Divide the dough into 12 pieces.
7. On a floured board, roll out each piece as thin as possible into rough 7¹/₂-inch circles.
8. Bake on griddle for 3 to 4 minutes, turning three or four times, until light brown.
9. Let cool completely before double-bagging in individual serving-sized bags.

Multigrain Sunflower Rolls

8 servings
Weight 1 serving (2 rolls) = 4 ounces

These rolls will keep for a week.
1. Place in a heavy bowl:
   > 1¹/₂ cups rolled oats
   > 2 tablespoons packed brown sugar
   > 1 tablespoon canola oil
   > 1 tablespoon dark molasses
   > ¹/₈ teaspoon salt
2. Add:
   > 1¹/₂ cups boiling water

   Stir; then cool for 20 minutes.
3. Mix together in a cup:
   > ³/₄ cup very warm water
   > 2 tablespoons (2 packages) active dry yeast

   Let stand for 20 minutes; then stir the yeast into the oat mixture.
4. Stir and knead in gradually:
   > 1 cup whole wheat flour
   > 1 cup unbleached white flour
   > ¹/₂ cup rye flour
   > ¹/₂ cup gluten flour
   > ¹/₄ cup hulled sunflower seeds
5. Cover and let rise in a warm place for 45 minutes, or until doubled in bulk.
6. Oil a baking sheet. Divide dough into 16 pieces. Shape into rolls and place them on the baking sheet. Let rise for 20 minutes.
7. Preheat oven to 350 degrees.
8. Bake rolls for 15 minutes. Let cool completely on wire racks before storing them in individual serving-sized bags.

Crackers

In your pack, safeguard crackers and other fragile foods from breakage. Pack them in clean recycled milk or oatmeal cartons (see chapter one).

Scottish Oaties

6 servings
Weight 1 serving (4 oaties) = 3 ounces

These are slightly sweet and excellent with cheese. They will keep for a week.
1. Mix together in a large bowl:
   1 1/2 cups whole wheat flour
   1/2 cup rolled oats
   1/4 cup packed brown sugar
   1/2 teaspoon baking powder
   1/4 teaspoon salt
2. Cut in:
   1/3 cup chilled butter or margarine
3. Stir in and blend well:
   1/2 cup cold water
4. Preheat oven to 350 degrees.
5. Scoop dough by the tablespoonful onto an ungreased baking sheet. Pat the oaties into 2 1/2-inch-diameter rounds. Bake for 12 to 15 minutes, or until light brown.
6. Let cool completely on wire racks before storing in individual serving-sized bags.

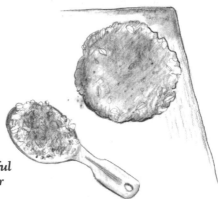

Scoop dough by the tablespoonful and pat into 2 1/2-inch-diameter rounds.

The following three traditional "rolled" cracker recipes make large quantities of crackers that will keep for six weeks or longer. If you don't have a rolling pin, use a clean, smooth-sided empty glass bottle. Be sure to package crackers in individual serving-sized bags for best quality during long storage.

Parmesan Cheese Crackers
7 servings
Weight 1 serving (15 crackers) = 2 ounces

Vary this recipe with other finely grated aged cheeses such as cheddar, Romano, or dry Jack.

1. Mix together in a large bowl:
    1 $^1/_2$ cups whole wheat flour
    $^1/_4$ cup unbleached white flour
    $^1/_4$ cup wheat germ
    1 tablespoon packed brown sugar
    1 teaspoon baking powder
    $^1/_2$ teaspoon salt
    $^1/_8$ teaspoon cayenne pepper
2. Cut in:
    $^1/_3$ cup chilled butter or margarine
    $^1/_2$ cup finely grated Parmesan cheese
    Stir in:
    $^1/_2$ cup cold water
3. Knead briefly; then turn the dough out onto a floured board.
4. Preheat oven to 350 degrees. Oil two large baking sheets.
5. Roll the dough as thin as possible on a floured board.
6. Cut the dough into 1-by-2$^1/_2$-inch rectangles; they do not need to be even. Prick the crackers all over with a fork to prevent buckling.
7. Place crackers on baking sheets. Bake for 5 minutes, or until lightly browned on bottoms.
8. Let cool completely on wire racks before storing in individual serving-sized bags.

Onion-Herb Crackers

These are different and delicious.

1. Mix together in a large bowl:

    1 1/2 cups whole wheat flour

    1/2 cup unbleached white flour

    6 tablespoons any mixed fresh herbs (thyme, parsley, basil, oregano), minced, or 3 tablespoons dried herbs

    3 scallions, minced

    2 tablespoons packed brown sugar

    1 teaspoon baking powder

    1/2 teaspoon salt

    1/4 teaspoon freshly ground black pepper

2. Cut in:

    1/3 cup chilled butter or margarine

    Stir in:

    1/2 cup cold water

3. Knead briefly; then turn the dough out onto a floured board. Roll the dough as thin as possible.

4. Preheat oven to 350 degrees. Oil two large baking sheets.

5. Sprinkle over the dough:

    1 tablespoon celery seed

    Roll the seed into the dough.

6. Using a knife, slice the dough into 1-by-2 1/2-inch rectangles; they do not need to be even. Prick them all over with a fork to prevent buckling.

7. Place crackers on the oiled baking sheets. Bake for 5 to 10 minutes, or until lightly browned on bottoms.

8. Let cool completely on wire racks before storing in individual serving-sized bags.

Sesame-Oat Crackers

7 servings
Weight 1 serving (15 crackers) = 2.5 ounces

These crackers are easy to make and keep a long time.

1. Mix together in a large bowl:

    1³/4 cups whole wheat flour
    ¹/4 cup unbleached white flour
    ¹/3 cup rolled oats, finely ground in a blender or food
       processor (¹/3 cup oat flour)
    1 tablespoon packed brown sugar
    1 teaspoon baking powder
    ¹/2 teaspoon salt
    1 tablespoon sesame seeds

2. Cut in:

    ¹/2 cup chilled butter or margarine

   Stir in:

    ¹/3 cup cold water

3. Knead the dough briefly; then turn it out onto a floured board.

4. Preheat oven to 350 degrees. Lightly oil two large baking sheets.

5. Roll dough as thin as possible. Cut the dough into 1-by-2¹/2-inch rectangles; they do not need to be even. Prick them all over with a fork to prevent buckling.

6. Place the crackers on the baking sheets. Bake for 5 minutes, or until lightly browned on bottoms.

7. Let cool completely on wire racks before storing in individual serving-sized bags.

Toasts

These breads are lightweight and they keep fresh up to 2 months.

Bagel Chips

4 servings
Weight 1 serving (1 bagel) = 3.5 ounces

These are simplicity itself.
1. Preheat oven to 375 degrees.
2. Slice, vertically, $^1/_8$ inch thick:
    4 day-old bagels, any variety
3. Place the slices in a single layer on ungreased baking sheets. Bake for 6 minutes; then turn the slices and bake 3 minutes longer, or until crisp and light brown.
4. Cool completely on wire racks before storing them in individual serving-sized bags.

Wheat Toasts

6 servings
Weight 1 serving (7 toasts) = 1.5 ounces

These are easy slice-and-bake toasts.
1. Mix together in a large bowl:
    $1^1/_2$ cups whole wheat flour
    $^1/_2$ cup toasted wheat germ
    3 tablespoons packed brown sugar
    1 teaspoon baking powder
    $^1/_2$ teaspoon salt
    $^1/_8$ teaspoon cayenne pepper
2. Cut in:
    $^1/_4$ cup butter or margarine
    Stir in:
    $^1/_2$ cup cold water
3. Knead briefly. Divide dough in half and roll into two logs $1^1/_2$ inches in diameter and $5^1/_2$ inches long. Cover and place in freezer for 1 hour. Remove from freezer.
4. Preheat oven to 400 degrees. Oil two baking sheets.

5. Slice logs ¹/₄ inch thick and place the slices on the baking sheets. Bake for 5 minutes, then turn and bake 5 minutes longer, or until light brown.
6. Let cool completely on wire racks before storing in individual serving-sized bags.

Whole-Grain Zwieback

8 servings
Weight 1 serving (4 slices) = 3 ounces

These twice-baked slices of wheat bread will keep for a whole season.
1. Preheat oven to 375 degrees. Oil a baking sheet.
2. Mix together in a large bowl:

> **2 cups whole wheat flour**
> **1 cup unbleached white flour**
> **¹/₄ cup wheat germ**
> **¹/₄ cup dry milk**
> **3 tablespoons brown sugar**
> **³/₄ teaspoon baking powder**
> **³/₄ teaspoon baking soda**
> **¹/₈ teaspoon salt**

3. Add and stir well:

> **1¹/₃ cups water**

4. Knead dough briefly on a well-floured board to form a round loaf. Place on baking sheet and cut a 1-inch-deep cross in the top.
5. Bake for 35 minutes or until loaf sounds hollow when tapped on bottom. Let cool completely on a wire rack.
6. Preheat oven to 200 degrees.
7. Slice loaf in half; then slice it crosswise into 3/8-inch-thick slices.
8. Place slices face down on an ungreased baking sheet. Bake for 30 minutes; then turn the slices over and bake 30 minutes longer.
9. Let cool completely on wire racks before storing in individual serving-sized bags.

Spreads

These truly instant spreads are dehydrated at home. At lunchtime, pour the dehydrated spread in your cup, add a little water, stir, and enjoy with crackers, chapatis, tortillas or tortilla chips, bread, zwieback, or rice cakes.

Backpack Bruschetta
4 servings, ²/₃ cup each
Weight 1 dried serving = 2 ounces

This savory spread is excellent when served with the preceding recipe for Whole-Grain Zwieback.
1. Purée in a blender or food processor:
   3 cloves garlic, minced
   15 ounces canned small white beans, rinsed and drained
   28 ounces canned crushed tomatoes
   juice of 1 fresh lemon (2 tablespoons juice)
   ¹/₄ teaspoon freshly ground black pepper
   ¹/₈ teaspoon salt
2. Spread on covered dehydrator trays and dehydrate for 4 hours at 145 degrees.
3. To rehydrate, add a little water, stirring until a thick spread consistency is obtained.

Quick Hummus
4 servings, ²/₃ cup each
Weight 1 dried serving = 3.5 ounces

This savory Middle-Eastern spread is easy to make.
1. Purée in a blender or food processor:
   3 cloves garlic, minced
   30 ounces canned garbanzo beans, drained, liquid
     reserved
   ¹/₂ cup toasted sesame seeds
   ¹/₄ cup olive oil
   juice of 1 fresh lemon (2 tablespoons juice)
   1 tablespoon minced fresh parsley leaves
   ¹/₂ teaspoon salt
   ¹/₄ teaspoon cayenne pepper
   Add small amounts of reserved bean liquid, if needed, to create a thick, smooth paste.

2. Spread on covered dehydrator trays and dehydrate for 3$^1/2$ hours at 145 degrees.
3. To rehydrate, add a little water, stirring, until dip or spread consistency is obtained. Serve with crackers, chapatis, tortilla chips, or pita bread.

White Bean Paté

4 servings, $^1/2$ cup each
Weight 1 dried serving = 3 ounces

This is an easy spread.
1. Heat a large skillet over medium heat. Add:
    1 tablespoon olive oil
When the oil is hot, add and sauté for 8 minutes:
    1 onion, diced
    1 carrot, diced
    3 cloves garlic, minced
    8 fresh mushrooms, diced
Add:
    $^1/2$ teaspoon salt
    $^1/8$ teaspoon cayenne pepper
2. Purée the vegetables in a blender or food processor, along with:
    30 ounces canned small white beans, rinsed and drained
3. Spread on covered dehydrator trays and dehydrate for 4$^1/2$ hours at 145 degrees.
4. To rehydrate, add a little water, stirring until spread consistency is obtained.

Curried Tofu Spread

4 servings, $^1/2$ cup each
Weight 1 dried serving = 2.5 ounces

This is different and delicious.
1. Heat a large skillet over medium-low heat. Add:
    1 tablespoon sesame oil
When the oil is hot, add:
    1 sweet onion, minced
    1 bell pepper, minced
    1 tablespoon curry powder
    $^1/8$ teaspoon cayenne pepper

3. Purée the vegetables in a blender or food processor, along with:

2 pounds tofu, crumbled

juice of 1 fresh lemon (2 tablespoons juice)

1 teaspoon salt

4. Spread on covered dehydrator trays and dehydrate for 5^1/2 hours at 145 degrees.

5. To serve, add a little water, stirring until spread consistency is obtained.

Some Like It Hot Bean Spread

4 servings, ^{2}/3 cup each
Weight 1 dried serving = 1.5 ounces

This is quick!

1. Purée in a blender or food processor:

30 ounces canned pinto beans, rinsed and drained

4 ounces canned diced green chilies

^{1}/2 cup salsa, mild, medium, or hot

^{1}/2 teaspoon salt

2. Spread on covered dehydrator trays and dehydrate for 4 hours at 145 degrees.

3. To rehydrate, add a little water, stirring until spread consistency is obtained. Serve with tortilla chips or with any variety bread.

Garbanzo Spread

4 servings, ^{1}/2 cup each
Weight 1 dried serving = 2 ounces

Garbanzo beans combine with peanut butter for a high-protein spread.

1. Purée in a blender or food processor:

2 scallions, minced

^{1}/2 teaspoon fresh thyme, minced, or ^{1}/4 teaspoon dried thyme

15 ounces canned garbanzo beans (chickpeas), plus liquid

^{1}/2 cup peanut butter

^{1}/3 cup orange, lemon, or other fruit juice

^{1}/2 teaspoon salt

^{1}/8 teaspoon cayenne pepper

2. Spread on covered dehydrator trays and dehydrate for 3^1/2 hours at 145 degrees.

3. To rehydrate, add a little water, stirring until spread consistency is obtained.

Creamy Tuna Spread

4 servings, ³/4 cup each
Weight 1 dried serving = 2 ounces

1. Purée in a blender or food processor:
     12 ounces water-packed canned tuna, drained
     30 ounces canned small white beans, rinsed and drained
     3 tablespoons salsa, mild, medium, or hot
     ¹/4 teaspoon salt
2. Spread on covered dehydrator trays and dehydrate for 3¹/2 hours at 145 degrees.
3. To rehydrate, add a little water, stirring until spread consistency is obtained.

Black Bean Salsa

4 servings, ²/3 cup each
Weight 1 dried serving = 2 ounces

1. Purée in a blender or food processor:
     5 cloves garlic, diced
     3 scallions, diced
     15 ounces canned black beans, rinsed and drained
     1 ripe avocado, peeled and pitted
     3 ripe tomatoes, chopped
     juice of 1 fresh lime (2 tablespoons juice)
     ¹/2 teaspoon chili powder
     ¹/4 teaspoon salt
2. Spread on covered dehydrator trays and dehydrate for 5 hours at 145 degrees.
3. To rehydrate, add a little water, stirring until spread consistency is obtained.

Jerky

Tasty, inexpensive jerky is very easy to make at home. Good jerky begins with very fresh fish or lean beef. Dry jerky quickly to avoid spoilage. Store home-dried jerky in the refrigerator for two months or in the freezer for six months. Keep it cool, dark, and dry on the trail and use it promptly.

Salmon Snack

10 servings
Weight 1 dried serving = 0.75 ounce

1. Mix together in a shallow glass dish:
   - $^1/_2$ cup tamari soy sauce
   - $^1/_2$ cup water
   - 1 tablespoon minced fresh ginger
   - $^1/_4$ teaspoon hot sauce
2. Wash and drain:
   - 1 pound uncooked skinless boneless salmon fillets
3. Slice the fish as thin as possible. Marinate the slices in the sauce for 15 minutes; then drain them in a colander.
4. Oil mesh dehydrator trays. Lay the fish slices directly on *uncovered* mesh dehydrator trays.
5. Dehydrate for 4 hours at 145 degrees, turning the slices once while drying.
6. When completely cool, place in individual serving-sized bags and store in refrigerator or freezer prior to your trip.

Fish Jerky

8 servings
Weight 1 dried serving = 1.5 ounces

1. Mix together in a large, shallow glass or ceramic dish:
   - $^1/_2$ cup water
   - $^1/_4$ cup tamari soy sauce
   - $^1/_4$ cup Worcestershire sauce
   - 2 tablespoons hot sauce
   - 1 teaspoon crushed red pepper flakes
2. Wash and drain in a colander:
   - 1 pound any uncooked skinless boneless fish fillets

3. Slice the fish as thin as possible. Marinate the slices in the sauce for 10 minutes; then drain in a colander.
4. Spray mesh dehydrator trays with vegetable oil. Place fish slices directly on *uncovered* mesh dehydrator trays.
5. Dehydrate for 6 hours at 145 degrees, turning the slices once after 2 hours.
6. When completely cool, store in refrigerator or freezer in individual serving-sized bags prior to your trip.

Beef Jerky

4 servings
Weight 1 dried serving = 1.5 ounces

This is easy and delicious.
1. Place in freezer until partially frozen:
    1 pound lean flank or round steak
2. Remove and discard fat.
3. Slice the meat into $1/4$-inch-thick strips.
4. Mix together in a large, shallow glass casserole dish:
    3 tablespoons tamari soy sauce
    3 tablespoons Worcestershire sauce
    1 tablespoon liquid smoke
    1 tablespoon chili powder
    1 teaspoon hot sauce
    2 cloves garlic, minced
5. Marinate the strips in the sauce, stirring to coat, for 3 minutes.
6. Oil mesh dehydrator trays. Lay the strips directly on *uncovered* mesh trays.
7. Dehydrate for 6 hours at 145 degrees, turning the strips once while drying.
8. When completely cool, store in refrigerator or freezer in individual serving-sized bags prior to your trip.

Variation

Leftover *cooked* chicken or turkey makes tasty, slightly chewy jerky. Slice the cooked meat as thin as possible, trimming away every bit of fat, and follow the above recipe for Beef Jerky. Pork, cooked or not, is not suitable for jerky.

CHAPTER THREE

SWEET AND SAVORY SNACKS

GORP (good old raisins and peanuts) will give you energy on the trail but so will many other, more imaginative, treats. Savory snacks such as roasted soybeans, walnuts, and savory split peas will provide variety. Healthy home-baked potato chips will surprise you with their light weight and simple preparation. A raw baking potato weighs about eight ounces; sliced and baked, a whole potato weighs only two ounces. Simple fruit snacks—sliced fruit and fruit leather—require no preservatives and can be home-dried year-round. To make fruit leather, simply purée sweetened fruit, or a combination of fruits, and pour onto covered dehydrator trays. Dry until firm; then roll up for a concentrated lightweight sweet snack.

Nuts, Beans, and Vegetables

Spiced Mixed Nuts

8 servings
Weight 1 serving ($^1/_2$ cup) = 4 ounces

These will keep for six weeks.
1. Toast in a large skillet over low heat for 3 minutes:
    $^1/_4$ **cup sesame seed**
   Add:
    2 tablespoons sesame oil
    $^1/_2$ **cup packed brown sugar**
    $^1/_2$ **teaspoon crushed red pepper flakes (hot) or** $^1/_2$ **tea-spoon paprika (mild)**
   Cook for 5 minutes, stirring occasionally.
2. Add and cook 3 minutes longer, or until brown and fragrant:
    4 cups unsalted mixed nuts
    1 tablespoon soy sauce
    $^1/_2$ **teaspoon liquid smoke**
3. Turn out onto a large baking sheet to cool completely before storing.

Savory Split Pea Snacks

9 servings
Weight 1 serving (¹/3 cup) = 3 ounces

These are a welcome change from the usual trail snacks.

1. Place in a large ceramic bowl:

   1³/4 cup dried split peas, rinsed and drained
   8 cups cold water
   1 tablespoon baking soda

   Let stand in a cool place for 12 to 24 hours, or until softened. Rinse the peas, drain them well in a colander, and then spread them on a towel to dry.
2. Preheat oven to 300 degrees.
3. Spread the peas on a rimmed baking sheet. Add and stir until coated:

   1 tablespoon olive oil

   Roast the peas for 20 minutes, stir, then roast 20 minutes longer.
4. Mix together in a paper bag:

   ³/4 teaspoon salt
   ¹/2 teaspoon ground cumin
   ¹/4 teaspoon cayenne pepper
   ¹/8 teaspoon ground ginger

   Place the peas in the bag while they are still warm. Twist top of bag and shake to coat peas with spices.
5. Let the peas cool completely before storing them in individual serving-sized bags.

Caramelized Walnuts

8 servings
Weight 1 serving (¹/2 cup) = 4 ounces

These are slightly sweet. They will keep in your pack for 3 weeks.

1. Blend in a large skillet over low heat:

   ¹/2 cup brown sugar
   1 tablespoon canola oil
   1 tablespoon soy sauce
2. Add and cook, stirring, for 5 minutes, or until brown and fragrant:

   4 cups walnut halves or pieces
3. Spread the nuts on a large baking sheet to cool completely before storing in individual serving-sized bags.

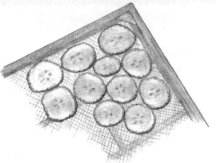

Zucchini Chips

Tomato or Zucchini Chips

Weight 1 dried serving (1 whole tomato or zucchini) = fraction of an ounce

1. Lightly brush or spray *uncovered* mesh dehydrator trays with vegetable oil.
2. Slice tomatoes or zucchini (or any summer squash) as thin as possible ($1/8$-inch to $1/4$-inch slices). One zucchini will fill one dehydrator tray; two tomatoes will fill one dehydrator tray. Place the slices on the drying trays in a single layer. Sprinkle with:
     seasoned salt or salt-free seasoning
3. Dehydrate for 2 hours for zucchini or 6 hours for tomatoes at 145 degrees, turning the slices once during drying. Dry until hard but pliable.

Marinated Vegetable Chips

Weight 1 dried serving (1 whole carrot, cucumber, zucchini, or pickle) = fraction of an ounce

1. Place in a large, shallow glass or pottery dish:
     $1/2$ cup any vinegar
     salt, pepper, and minced herbs to taste
   Add:
     unpeeled carrots, zucchini, or tomatoes, or peeled
     cucumbers, sliced as thin as possible
   Set aside to marinate for 5 minutes.
2. Drain the vegetables in a colander and place them on *uncovered*, oiled mesh dehydrator trays.

3. Dehydrate at 145 degrees for 3 to 5 hours or until crisp, turning them once during drying.

Time-saving tips: Substitute any thinly sliced commercial pickles for the marinated vegetables. Sour dill pickles make a tasty dried treat.

When fresh vegetables are in season, make good use of the produce from your garden or the farmers' market. Wash and thinly slice cucumbers, any summer squash, Jerusalem artichokes, onions, bell peppers, or scallions. Place the slices in very clean glass jars. Cover the sliced vegetables with vinegar and fresh herbs. Cover and store in the refrigerator for 6 months or longer. They can be used fresh as refrigerator pickles or can be dehydrated at your convenience.

Baked Potato Chips

2 servings
Weight 1 dried serving (1 potato) = 2 ounces

These are easy to make and delightfully not greasy.
1. Preheat oven to 350 degrees.
2. Lightly oil two large baking sheets.
3. Cut into $^1/_{16}$-inch-thick slices:
   2 large baking potatoes, scrubbed but not peeled
   Place the slices in a single layer on the baking sheets. Sprinkle them with:
   $^1/_2$ teaspoon salt
   $^1/_4$ teaspoon ground white pepper
4. Bake for 20 to 30 minutes, or until golden brown, turning them once while baking.
5. Let cool completely before storing them in individual serving-sized bags.

Variation: Spicy Potato Chips
Along with the salt and pepper, sprinkle the potato slices with:
   $^1/_8$ teapoon cayenne pepper
   $^1/_4$ teaspoon chili powder

Slice whole potatoes into $^1/_{16}$-inch-thick slices.

Roasted Soybeans

8 servings
Weight 1 serving (4 tablespoons) = 2 ounces

These are mild, crisp, and nutty.

1. Place in a large saucepan:

   2 cups dried soybeans, rinsed and drained
   6 cups water

   Bring to a boil; then reduce heat and simmer for 10 minutes. Turn off heat and let beans stand in the cooking water, covered, for 2 hours.
2. Preheat oven to 450 degrees.
3. Rinse and drain the beans. Spread them in a single layer on a rimmed baking sheet. Sprinkle over the beans and stir to coat:

   1 tablespoon olive oil
   1 tablespoon chili powder or curry powder
   1 1/2 teaspoons salt
4. Bake for 80 minutes, stirring occasionally, until beans are crisp and brown.
5. Let cool completely before storing in individual serving-sized bags.

Pecan Caramel Corn

8 servings
Weight 1 serving (1 1/2 cups) = 2 ounces

1. Heat a covered Dutch oven over medium heat. Add:

   3 tablespoons canola oil

   When the oil is hot, add, stirring to coat:

   3/4 cup popcorn

   Cover and cook, shaking the pot occasionally, until corn has stopped popping.
2. Gently melt together in a small saucepan:

   3/4 cup corn syrup
   1/2 cup packed brown sugar
   2 tablespoons butter or margarine
   1 teaspoon vanilla extract
   1 cup pecan halves or pieces
   1 teaspoon salt
   1/4 teaspoon cayenne pepper
3. Preheat oven to 200 degrees. Oil a 10-by-13-inch glass casserole dish.

4. Spread the cooked popcorn in the casserole dish. Pour the sugar mixture over the warm popped corn. Stir to coat well.
5. Bake for 1 hour, stirring every 20 minutes.
6. Let cool completely before storing in individual serving-sized bags.

Dried Fruit and Fruit Leather

The absence of sulfur or other chemicals makes your own simple home-dried ripe fruit taste far better than commercially dried treated fruit. Another advantage is that you can dry fruit to just the stage of toothsome chewiness that you prefer. For the finest raisins you've ever tasted, wash, then dehydrate whole seedless grapes until dry but still soft.

Fruit leather is easy to make. Purée very ripe fruit in a blender, food processor, or food mill until it is thick but still pourable. If the puréed fruit is too thin, strain off some of the juice. If the purée is too thick, add a small amount of any fruit juice. The purée should be about $1/4$ inch thick when it is poured onto covered dehydrator trays. Dry until leathery: pliable but with no sticky spots. Roll up the leather while it is still warm; then cut the roll into snack-sized pieces (one quarter of a roll) for enjoyment on the trail.

Apple Leather

32 servings
Weight 1 dried serving = 0.5 ounce

1. Wash and cut in half:

   5 pounds whole apples, seeds, cores, and stems included
   Put the apples in a large pot. Cover with:
   1 cup water

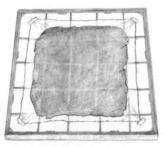

Pour puréed fruit onto covered dehydrator trays.

2. Bring to a boil, then reduce heat and cook, stirring occasionally, for 30 minutes, or until apples are tender.
3. To remove seeds, stems, and skins, strain the apples and juice through a food mill or strainer into a large bowl. Stir in:

   ¹/₄ cup brown sugar
   ¹/₂ teaspoon cinnamon
4. Oil covered dehydrator trays with vegetable oil. Spread the apple leather in even 8-inch-diameter circles on the trays.
5. Dehydrate at 145 degrees for 6 hours or until firm and leathery.
6. Roll up the leather while it is still warm; then cut each roll into 4 pieces. Let cool completely before storing in individual serving-sized bags.

Time-saving tip: Purchase commercially made applesauce. Stir in flavoring, such as a sprinkle of cinnamon, if desired. Pour 1 cup of applesauce on each covered, oiled dehydrator tray. (1 cup applesauce = one 8-inch-diameter roll).

Cherry Leather
32 servings
Weight 1 dried serving = 0.5 ounce

1. Wash and remove stems and stones from:

   3 pounds (10 cups) ripe fresh cherries

   Purée the cherries in a blender or food processor, along with:

   ¹/₂ cup white corn syrup
   ¹/₂ teaspoon ground cinnamon
2. Heat the cherry purée in a medium saucepan just until boiling.
3. Oil covered dehydrator trays with vegetable oil. Pour the purée onto the trays in even 8-inch-diameter circles.
4. Dehydrate at 135 degrees for 7 to 10 hours, or until firm but leathery.
5. Roll up the leather while it is still warm; then cut each roll into 4 pieces. Let cool completely before storing in individual serving-sized bags.

Roll, and then slice into quarters.

Spring Strawberry Leather

32 servings
Weight 1 dried serving = 0.5 ounce

This is the essence of strawberry flavor.
1. Wash, rubbing off seeds, then core and drain in a colander:
   3 pounds (10 cups) ripe fresh strawberries
   Purée the strawberries in a blender or food processor, along with:
   ¹/₂ cup white corn syrup
   ¹/₂ teaspoon ground ginger
2. Oil covered dehydrator trays with vegetable oil. Pour the purée onto the trays in even 8-inch-diameter circles.
3. Dehydrate at 135 degrees for 7 to 10 hours, or until firm but leathery.
4. Roll up the leather while it is still warm; then cut each roll into 4 pieces. Let cool completely before storing in individual serving-sized bags.

Fruit Leather Variations

Try the following fruits:
   unpeeled apricots, peaches, pears, or plums
   peeled nectarines or pineapple
   Use 10 cups of fresh fruit. Choose one fruit or a combination of several fruits. Purée the fruit along with a small amount of honey, sugar, or corn syrup, plus spice to taste.
   For additional variety, sprinkle over the fruit leather before putting it into the dehydrator:

any variety finely chopped nuts	**flaked coconut**
any variety hulled seeds	**granola cereal**

Banana Chips

Weight 1 dried serving (1 banana) = 1.5 ounces

1. Lightly oil *uncovered* mesh dehydrator trays with vegetable oil.
2. Peel, then cut into ¹/₈- to ¹/₄-inch-thick slices:
   ripe bananas
   Place in a single layer directly on mesh dehydrator trays. Two bananas will fill three dehydrator trays.
3. Dehydrate at 145 degrees for 5 hours, or until firm and leathery.
4. Let cool completely before storing in individual serving-sized bags.

Trail Mixes

The same trail mix day after day becomes tiresome. Instead, vary your snack combinations. Pack individual serving-sized bags of two, three, or more of the following choices. Plan different combinations for each day. Adventurous snackers can combine sweet choices with savory ones.

Sweet Trail Mix Choices

Any small, chewy candies
Chocolate, carob, or butterscotch chips
Chopped dried fruit
Raisins
Chocolate-covered raisins
Shredded coconut
Any variety ready-to-eat cereal

Savory Trail Mix Choices

Popped corn
Mini pretzels, crackers, bagel chips, or rice cakes
Grated hard natural aged cheese
Dried vegetable chips
Any variety shelled nuts
Shelled sunflower or pumpkin seeds
Brewer's yeast
Toasted wheat germ
Crumbled jerky
Chow mein noodles

Bars and Cookies

Puma Bars

8 servings
Weight 1 serving (1 bar) = 4 ounces

1. Preheat oven to 350 degrees. Oil a 10-by-6-inch baking pan.
2. Heat in a large, heavy saucepan over medium heat:
    $^1/_3$ cup canola oil
   When the oil is hot, add:
    $^2/_3$ cup pecan pieces
   Cook, stirring, for 3 minutes, or until light brown. Remove from heat.
3. Add and beat well:
    $1^1/_4$ cups packed brown sugar
    $1^1/_2$ teaspoons vanilla extract
    2 eggs
    $^3/_4$ cup whole wheat flour
    $^1/_4$ cup unbleached white flour
    2 tablespoons wheat germ
    1 teaspoon baking powder
    1 cup butterscotch morsels
4. Pour into pan and bake for 18 minutes, or until just set. Cool completely on a wire rack before cutting into 8 bars. Store bars in individual serving-sized bags.

Pecan Shortbread

8 servings
Weight 1 serving (1 bar) = 1.5 ounces

1. Preheat oven to 325 degrees. Spread on a rimmed baking sheet:
    1 cup pecans
   Bake the pecans for 7 minutes, stirring occasionally.
2. Finely grind the pecans in a blender or food processor.
3. Cream together in a large bowl:
    $^1/_2$ cup butter
    $^3/_4$ cup confectioners' sugar
    $^1/_2$ teaspoon vanilla extract
   Beat in the ground pecans and:
    1 cup whole wheat flour

4. Oil a 6-by-10-inch baking pan. Pat the dough evenly into the pan. Using a fork, deeply score the dough into 8 bars.
5. Bake for 15 minutes, or until light brown.
6. Let cool completely, then cut along score lines. Store in individual serving-sized bags.

Blueberry Jamwiches

30 servings
Weight 1 serving (2 jamwiches) = 2.5 ounces

1. Beat together in a large bowl:
   1 cup butter or margarine, softened
   1¹/₄ cups packed brown sugar
   1 egg
   1¹/₂ teaspoons vanilla extract
   Add and mix well:
   2¹/₂ cups whole wheat flour
   ¹/₄ cup wheat germ
   ¹/₂ teaspoon baking powder
2. Shape the dough into a 16-inch-long roll. Wrap and refrigerate for 2 hours.
3. Preheat oven to 350 degrees.
4. Cut dough crosswise into ¹/₄-inch-thick slices. Place on ungreased baking sheets and bake for 8 minutes, or until light brown. Let cool completely on wire racks.
5. Spread evenly on half of the cookies:
   blueberry or other variety preserves, 1 scant teaspoon
      per cookie
   Top the preserve-covered cookies with the remaining cookies.
6. Store in individual serving-sized bags.

Oatmeal-Sesame Cookies

15 servings
Weight 1 serving (3 cookies) = 1.5 ounces

These keep for six weeks or longer.

1. Toast in a skillet over low heat, stirring frequently, for 8 minutes, or until light brown:

    ³/4 cup sesame seeds
    ³/4 cup flaked coconut
    ³/4 cup rolled oats

    Remove from heat and set aside.
2. Preheat oven to 325 degrees.
3. Beat together in a large bowl:

    1 egg
    ³/4 cup canola oil
    ³/4 cup honey
    1 teaspoon vanilla extract
4. Stir in and blend well:

    2 cups whole wheat flour
    ¹/2 teaspoon baking powder
    ¹/2 teaspoon baking soda
5. Blend in the toasted seed and oat mixture.
6. After dipping your hands in cold water, roll the dough into balls the size of walnuts. Place them 2 inches part on ungreased baking sheets. Flatten the cookies with a fork dipped in cold water.
7. Bake for 6 minutes, or until light brown.
8. Let cool completely on wire racks before storing in individual serving-sized bags.

Indian Heaven Snacks

20 servings
Weight 1 serving (3 balls) = 3 ounces

No baking is needed to make these high-energy treats. They will keep fresh for more than a month.

1. Toast in a small skillet until lightly browned:

    ¹/2 cup sesame seeds

    Set aside.
2. Bring to a boil in a large skillet over medium heat:

    ¹/2 cup packed brown sugar   **2 tablespoons canola oil**
    ¹/2 cup honey   **¹/2 cup water**

    Reduce heat and simmer for 2 minutes.

3. Remove from heat. Stir in and mix thoroughly:
   > 1 cup peanut butter
   > $^1/_2$ cup whole wheat flour
   > $2^1/_2$ cups rolled oats
   > $^1/_2$ cup wheat germ
   > $1^1/_2$ cups any variety finely chopped nuts
4. Roll into balls the size of small walnuts; then roll them in the toasted sesame seeds.
5. Set on plates, cover, and chill in refrigerator for several hours, or until they are firm. Store in individual serving-sized bags at room temperature.

Almond Biscotti

15 servings
Weight 1 serving (3 slices) = 3 ounces

1. Preheat oven to 350 degrees. Oil a large baking sheet.
2. Beat together in a medium bowl:
   > $^1/_4$ cup canola oil
   > 4 eggs
   > 1 cup brown sugar
   > 1 teaspoon almond or vanilla extract
3. Stir in and blend well:
   > $2^1/_2$ cups whole wheat flour
   > 1 teaspoon baking powder
   > 1 teaspoon baking soda
   > 1 teaspoon ground cinnamon
   > $^1/_2$ teaspoon ground nutmeg
   > $1^1/_2$ cups almonds, finely chopped
4. Mound the dough into two 11-inch-long logs on the baking sheet.
5. Bake for 15 minutes, or until very light brown.
6. Remove from oven. Let cool on baking sheet for 1 hour.
7. Preheat oven to 350 degrees. Cut logs into $^1/_2$-inch-thick slices. Place slices, face down, in a single layer on the baking sheet and bake for 10 minutes. Turn the slices and bake them 5 minutes longer, or until crisp and light brown.
8. Cool completely on wire racks before storing in individual serving-sized bags.

Haystacks

8 servings
Weight 1 serving (3 pieces) = 2 ounces

These are crunchy and different.

1. Melt in the top of a double boiler:

     8 ounces white baking chocolate

   Stir in:

     1 cup any variety chopped nuts
     2 cups chow mein noodles

2. Blend well; then drop the warm mixture by the tablespoonful onto waxed paper. Cover and refrigerate for 2 hours or until firm.

3. Store in individual serving-sized bags at room temperature.

Peanut Butter Fudge

20 servings
Weight 1 serving (3 balls) = 2 ounces

1. Mix together in a large bowl:

     1 cup peanut butter
     ³/4 cup honey

   Stir in:

     1 cup instant dry milk
     1 cup confectioners' sugar, sifted

2. Roll into balls the size of small walnuts; then roll them in:

     ¹/2 cup dry roasted peanuts, chopped

3. Place on a platter in a single layer, cover, and refrigerate for 2 hours.

4. Store in individual serving-sized bags at room temperature.

Roll the fudge in chopped peanuts.

Chocolate Treats

1. Toast in a skillet over medium heat for 3 minutes, or until light brown:

    1 cup rolled oats

    Set aside.
2. Melt in the top of a double boiler over hot, but not boiling, water:

    1 pound bittersweet baking chocolate
    1 cup honey
3. Stir in the rolled oats and:

    3 cups puffed rice cereal
    1 cup any variety finely chopped nuts
4. Roll into balls the size of walnuts. Place in a shallow bowl:

    2 cups flaked coconut

    Roll the balls in the coconut.
5. Let cool completely; then store in individual serving-sized bags at room temperature.

White Chocolate Granola Bars

1. Oil a 6-by-10-inch glass baking dish.
2. Melt in the top of a double boiler:

    12 ounces white baking chocolate
    ³/4 cup light corn syrup
3. Stir in:

    3 cups any variety granola
4. Spread evenly in oiled dish. Let cool comletely before cutting into 12 bars. Store in individual serving-sized bags.

No-Bake Brandy Delights

20 servings
Weight 1 serving (3 pieces) = 2 ounces

Enjoy the alpenglow with these after-dinner treats.

1. Mix together in a large bowl:

    30 graham crackers, finely crushed (about 6 cups crushed)

    2 cups confectioners' sugar

    1/4 cup pecans, finely ground

    1/2 cup light corn syrup

    2/3 cup brandy

2. Roll the dough into balls the size of walnuts. Store in individual serving-sized bags at room temperature.

CHAPTER FOUR

SOUPS AND STEWS

It's deep in December. You have just cooked a big, steaming pot of Black-Eyed Pea Soup. Enjoy some for dinner tonight; put the rest in the dehydrator. You will savor the soup again in July while camped on the shoulder of a scenic mountain peak. To enjoy big portions of lightweight hot meals on the trail, try some of the following recipes. These soups are hearty and make complete meals in themselves. Soups, stews, pilafs, baked beans, and chili dehydrate lightweight and compact—and they rehydrate easily. Be sure to slice, grate, or dice the ingredients into small pieces, or purée the soup in a blender or food processor, before dehydrating it. Thick soups dehydrate easily, but even the thinnest broth dehydrates well, too. A good soup begins with a good stock.

About Stocks

A good-flavored stock makes a tastier, more nutritious soup or stew. You can use commercial beef, chicken, or vegetable stock or easily make your own.

To make your own instant stock, keep the ingredients handy in your freezer. Place all of your daily kitchen scraps in a large plastic bag or freezer container. Include bones or shells from meats, poultry, fish, or shellfish and skins or stems of any vegetables or herbs. Some wonderful choices are onion skins, celery or parsley ends and leaves, bits of tomato or mushroom, poultry bones, and shrimp shells. Store the scraps in your freezer and add to your store daily.

When you are ready to make stock, place all or part of the frozen scraps in a soup pot. Cover them with plenty of water, bring to a boil, and then simmer for thirty minutes for all-vegetable stock or one to two hours for meat or seafood stock. Let it cool; then strain it. Use immediately, or store in the refrigerator for up to five days.

Use care when adding pepper stems and seeds to your stock store; sweet pepper parts can make the stock bitter, and hot peppers can make an extremely hot stock. Some vegetables simply taste stronger than others. Cabbage parts are delicious in stock, but can make its flavor overpowering. Taste your stock before using it in a soup or stew; thin an overly hot or strong-flavored stock with water.

Soups

Peanut Soup

Serves 4
Weight 1 dried serving = 4 ounces

1. Heat a Dutch oven over medium-low heat. Add:

    1 tablespoon peanut oil

    When the oil is hot, add:

    1 onion, minced
    1 bell pepper, minced
    2 cloves garlic, minced

    Cook for 5 minutes, stirring occasionally.

2. Add and bring to a boil:

    6 cups any variety stock

    Stir in:

    1 cup whole wheat couscous
    $^1/_2$ cup TVP (textured vegetable protein)

    Reduce heat, add and simmer for 5 minutes:

    4 tablespoons chunky peanut butter
    4 ounces canned diced green chilies
    2 tablespoons hot sauce
    1 teaspoon salt

3. Spread on covered dehydrator trays and dehydrate for 5 hours at 145 degrees.

4. To rehydrate, cover with water $1^1/_2$ inches above level of food in pot, boil, stir, and serve.

Tomato Pea Soup

1. Place in a large pot:
   1³/4 cups dried split peas, washed and drained
   10 cups any variety stock or water
   Let stand for 1 hour.
2. Add and bring to a boil:
   1 small onion or 1 large leek, minced
   2 carrots, diced
   3 stalks celery, diced
   3 cloves garlic, minced
   28 ounces canned crushed tomatoes
   1 sprig fresh thyme or 1 teaspoon dried thyme
   1 whole bay leaf
   1 tablespoon honey
   1 teaspoon olive oil
   Reduce heat and simmer, covered, for 3 hours.
3. Remove bay leaf and thyme sprig. Stir in and cook 5 minutes longer:
   1 cup TVP (textured vegetable protein)
4. Remove from heat and stir in:
   ¹/2 cup dry sherry
   1 teaspoon salt
   2 tablespoons hot sauce
   1 cup finely grated Parmesan cheese
5. Purée the soup in a blender or food processor.
6. Spread on covered dehydrator trays and dehydrate for 6¹/2 hours at 145 degrees.
7. To rehydrate, cover with water 2 inches above level of food in pot, boil, stir, and serve.

Legume-Salami Soup

Serves 4
Weight 1 dried serving = 5.5 ounces

1. Rinse, drain, and place in a large pot:

   1 cup dried lentils
   1 cup dried split peas

   Add:

   7 cups water

   Bring to a boil; then reduce heat and simmer, covered, for 40 minutes.

2. Put the soup in a blender or food processor along with the following, coarsely chopped:

   8 ounces salami
   1 onion
   1 carrot
   2 stalks celery
   ¹/₂ cup parsley leaves
   3 cloves garlic

   Add:

   1 tablespoon olive oil
   1 tablespoon honey

   Purée until smooth.

3. Return the soup to the pot. Add:

   3 cups water

   Bring to a boil; then reduce heat to very low and simmer for 10 minutes, stirring occasionally.

4. Stir in:

   ¹/₄ cup red wine
   ¹/₂ teaspoon salt
   ¹/₂ teaspoon cayenne pepper

5. Spread on covered dehydrator trays and dehydrate for 6 hours at 145 degrees.

6. To rehydrate, cover with water 1¹/₂ inches above level of food in pot, boil, stir, and serve.

Bean and Pasta Soup

Serves 4
Weight 1 dried serving = 5.5 ounces

1. Cook, then drain in a colander:
    10 ounces vermicelli pasta, broken in thirds
    Return pasta to pot and set aside.
2. Heat a Dutch oven over medium-low heat. Add:
    1 tablespoon olive oil
    When the oil is hot, add:
    1 onion, minced
    1 large baking potato, scrubbed but not peeled, grated
    **1 teaspoon minced fresh rosemary or $^1/_2$ teaspoon dried
        rosemary**
    Cook, stirring occasionally, for 7 minutes.
3. Add:
    14 ounces canned peeled Italian plum tomatoes, crushed
    15 ounces canned kidney beans, rinsed and drained
    3 cups any variety stock
    1 teaspoon salt
    $^1/_2$ teaspoon freshly ground black pepper
    Cook 5 minutes longer, then stir in the cooked pasta.
4. Spread on covered dehydrator trays and dehydrate for 6 hours at
    145 degrees.
5. To rehydrate, cover with water 1 inch above level of food in pot,
    boil, stir, and serve.

Cheddar Soup Plus

Serves 4
Weight 1 dried serving = 5 ounces

1. Heat a Dutch oven over medium-low heat. Add:
    2 tablespoons olive oil
    When the oil is hot, add:
    1 onion, minced
    6 stalks celery, minced
    2 carrots, minced
    Cook, stirring occasionally, for 5 minutes.

2. Stir in:
>   1/3 cup whole wheat flour

Add slowly:
>   7 cups chicken or vegetable stock

Bring to a boil, then add:
>   3/4 cup whole wheat couscous
>   3/4 cup TVP (textured vegetable protein)

Reduce heat to very low and cook, covered, 5 minutes.

3. Whisk in slowly, stirring constantly:
>   1/2 cup milk
>   1 tablespoon ground mustard
>   1 tablespoon hot sauce

4. Remove pot from heat. Cool for 1 minute, then stir in:
>   1 1/2 teaspoons salt
>   1/4 cup dry sherry
>   1 cup grated cheddar cheese
>   1/2 cup finely grated Parmesan cheese

5. Spread on covered dehydrator trays and dehydrate for 6 1/2 hours at 145 degrees.

6. To rehydrate, cover with water 1/2 inch above level of food in pot, boil, stir, and serve.

Carrot Soup

Serves 4
Weight 1 dried serving = 4 ounces

---

1. Heat a Dutch oven over medium heat. Add:
>   1 tablespoon olive oil

When the oil is hot, add and cook for 15 minutes, stirring occasionally:
>   1 onion, chopped
>   6 carrots, scrubbed but not peeled, chopped
>   5 fresh mushrooms, chopped
>   1 zucchini, chopped

2. Add and bring to a boil:
>   6 cups any variety stock
>   3/4 cup dried lentils
>   1/2 cup uncooked brown rice

Reduce heat and simmer, covered, for 50 minutes, or until rice and lentils are tender.

Use fresh carrots and mushrooms.

3. Stir in:
   > 1 teaspoon honey
   > 1 teaspoon salt
   > $^1/_2$ teaspoon ground ginger
   > $^1/_2$ teaspoon ground turmeric
   > $^1/_4$ teaspoon ground nutmeg
   > 1 tablespoon hot sauce
4. Purée the soup in a blender or food processor.
5. Spread on covered dehydrator trays and dehydrate for 6 hours at 145 degrees.
6. To rehydrate, cover with water 2 inches above level of food in pot, boil, stir, and serve.

Caldo Verde

Serves 4
Weight 1 dried serving = 4 ounces

This is Portugal's classic green soup.
1. Cover and bring to a boil; then simmer for 20 minutes, or until soft:
   > 14 ounces canned chicken broth
   > 3 cups water
   > 9 red potatoes (about 2$^1/_2$ pounds), scrubbed but not peeled, cut into 1-inch chunks

2. Crush the potatoes along with the liquid in the pot using a potato masher or fork. Add to the pot:

   1 teaspoon olive oil
   1 onion, minced
   2 cloves garlic, minced
   10 kale leaves, ribs removed, very finely shredded
   15 ounces canned small white beans, rinsed and drained
   $^1/_2$ teaspoon salt
   $^1/_4$ teaspoon freshly ground black pepper

   Bring to a boil and cook 15 minutes longer.
3. Spread on covered dehydrator trays and dehydrate for 6 hours at 145 degrees.
4. To rehydrate, cover with water 2 inches above level of food in pot, boil, stir, and serve.

Potluck Pass Potage

Serves 4
Weight 1 dried serving = 3 ounces

This featherweight, filling soup offers infinite seasonal variety.

1. Heat a Dutch oven over low heat. Add:

   1 tablespoon olive oil

   When the oil is hot, add:

   9 cups any finely diced vegetables (onions, garlic, zucchini, green beans, peas, carrots, cabbage, celery, broccoli, cauliflower, mushrooms, potatoes, corn, eggplant)

   Cook, stirring occasionally, for 20 minutes.
2. Add:

   2 tablespoons fresh or 1 tablespoon dried herbs, chopped
   5 cups vegetable, chicken, or beef stock
   $^1/_2$ cup whole wheat couscous
   $^1/_2$ cup TVP (textured vegetable protein)

   Cover and bring to a boil; then reduce heat and simmer, stirring occasionally, for 30 minutes.

   Stir in:

   1 tablespoon salt
   1 tablespoon Worcestershire sauce
   3 tablespoons hot sauce

3. Spread on covered dehydrator trays and dehydrate for 7 hours at 145 degrees.
4. To rehydrate, cover with water 1^1/2 inches above level of food in pot, boil, stir, and serve.

Pistou

Serves 4
Weight 1 dried serving = 5 ounces

This vegetable soup offers a taste of the south of France.

1. Place in a large saucepan:
> **4 medium red potatoes (about 1^1/2 pounds), scrubbed but not peeled, diced**
> **12 green beans, diced**
> **5 cups water**

Bring to a boil; then simmer, covered, for 20 minutes.

2. Add:
> **28 ounces canned crushed tomatoes**

Bring to a boil and add:
> **6 ounces vermicelli pasta, broken in thirds**

Bring to a boil; then reduce heat and cook 12 minutes longer, or until pasta is just tender.

3. Purée in a blender or food processor:
> **1 tablespoon olive oil**
> **1 tablespoon water**
> **1 bunch fresh basil leaves**
> **^{1}/2 cup finely grated Parmesan cheese**
> **3 cloves garlic**
> **1 tablespoon hot sauce**
> **1 teaspoon salt**

4. Stir the basil mixture into the soup.
5. Spread on covered dehydrator trays and dehydrate for 5^1/2 hours at 145 degrees.
6. To rehydrate, cover with water 1^1/2 inches above level of food in pot, boil, stir, and serve.

Garlic-Bean Soup
Serves 4
Weight 1 dried serving = 5 ounces

1. Heat a Dutch oven over medium-low heat. Add:
      1 tablespoon olive oil
   When the oil is hot, add and cook for 5 minutes, stirring occasionally:
      2 onions, minced
      15 cloves garlic, minced
2. Add and bring to a boil:
      15 ounces canned small white beans, rinsed and drained
      14 ounces canned chicken broth
      2 cups water
3. Add and simmer for 5 minutes:
      1¹/₂ cups (10 ounces) orzo (barley-shaped) pasta
4. Stir in:
      12 ounces canned evaporated milk
      ¹/₂ teaspoon salt
      ¹/₄ teaspoon ground white pepper
5. Spread on covered dehydrator trays and dehydrate for 5 hours at 145 degrees.
6. To rehydrate, cover with water 1¹/₂ inches above level of food in pot, boil, stir, and serve.

Sweet Potato Lentil Soup
Serves 4
Weight 1 dried serving = 4 ounces

1. Rinse and drain and place in a medium saucepan:
      ²/₃ cup dried lentils
   Cover with:
      2 cups water
   Bring to a boil; then simmer, covered, for 30 minutes, or until tender.
2. Meanwhile, cut into quarters and place in a large saucepan:
      3 sweet potatoes, scrubbed but not peeled
      2 onions, peeled
   Cover with:
      6 cups of water
   Bring to a boil; then simmer, covered, for 20 minutes.

3. Purée the potatoes, onions, lentils, and their cooking waters in a blender or food processor along with:

> 1 teaspoon salt
> 1/2 teaspoon cayenne pepper
> 1/4 teaspoon ground nutmeg

4. Spread on covered dehydrator trays and dehydrate for 6 1/2 hours at 145 degrees.
5. To rehydrate, cover with water 2 inches above level of food in pot, boil, stir, and serve.

Chickpea–Brown Rice Soup
Serves 4
Weight 1 dried serving = 4 ounces

---

1. Bring to a boil in a large pot:

> 3/4 cup uncooked brown rice, rinsed and drained
> 4 1/2 cups vegetable, beef, or chicken stock
> 1 whole bay leaf
> 1 teaspoon fresh thyme, minced, or 1/2 teaspoon dried thyme

Reduce heat and simmer, covered, for 35 minutes, or until rice is tender.

2. Add and cook 15 minutes longer:

> 15 ounces canned garbanzo beans (chickpeas), rinsed and drained
> 1 onion, minced
> 3 cloves garlic, minced
> 28 ounces canned crushed tomatoes

Remove the bay leaf. Stir in:

> 1 teaspoon salt
> 1/4 teaspoon cayenne pepper

3. Purée the soup in a blender or food processor.
4. Spread on covered dehydrator trays and dehydrate for 5 hours at 145 degrees.
5. To rehydrate, cover with water 1 1/2 inches above level of food in pot, boil, stir, and serve.

Potato Soup Parmesan

Serves 4
Weight 1 dried serving = 3.5 ounces

1. Cut into quarters and place in a large saucepan:
   4 medium baking potatoes (about 2 pounds), peeled
   1 onion, peeled
   Cover with:
   6 cups any variety stock or water
   Bring to a boil. Stir in:
   1 cup TVP (textured vegetable protein)
   Reduce heat and simmer, covered, for 20 mintues.
2. Mash the potato mixture along with the stock in the saucepan using a potato masher or fork. Stir in:
   12 ounces canned evaporated milk
   1^1/$_2$ teaspoons salt
   1 teaspoon freshly ground black pepper
3. Remove from heat and let cool for 1 minute. Stir in:
   ^{1}/$_2$ cup finely grated Parmesan cheese
4. Spread on covered dehydrator trays and dehydrate for 6^1/$_2$ hours at 145 degrees.
5. To rehydrate, cover with water ^{1}/$_2$ inch above level of food in pot, boil, stir, and serve.

White Bean Soup

Serves 4
Weight 1 dried serving = 4.5 ounces

1. Heat a Dutch oven over medium-low heat. Add:
   2 tablespoons olive oil
   When the oil is hot, add:
   ^{1}/$_2$ cup whole wheat flour
   5 cloves garlic, minced
   Stir for 3 minutes.
2. Add slowly, stirring constantly:
   12 ounces canned evaporated milk
   1 cup water
   45 ounces canned small white beans, rinsed, drained, and
   puréed in a blender or food processor
   ^{1}/$_2$ teaspoon salt
   ^{1}/$_4$ teaspoon freshly ground black pepper

Simmer for 2 minutes; then remove from heat and stir in:
>   1/2 cup finely grated Parmesan cheese
3. Spread on covered dehydrator trays and dehydrate for 4¹/2 hours at
   145 degrees.
4. To rehydrate, cover with water 1¹/2 inches above level of food in pot,
   boil, stir, and serve.

Sweet Onion Soup

Serves 4
Weight 1 dried serving = 4.5 ounces

---

1. Place in a bowl:
>   1 cup uncooked bulgur wheat

   Pour over it:
>   2 cups boiling water

   Cover and let stand for 30 minutes; then fluff with a fork.
2. Heat a Dutch oven over medium-low heat. Add:
>   1 tablespoon olive oil

   When the oil is hot, add:
>   2 large sweet white onions (about 2 pounds), minced
>   3 cloves garlic, minced

   Cook for 10 minutes, stirring occasionally.
3. Stir in the bulgur and add:
>   15 ounces canned garbanzo beans (chickpeas), rinsed
>   and drained
>   12 ounces canned evaporated milk
>   1 teaspoon salt
>   1/4 teaspoon cayenne pepper
>   1/8 teaspoon ground nutmeg
4. Purée the soup in a blender or food processor.
5. Spread on covered dehydrator trays and dehydrate for 5 hours at
   145 degrees.
6. To rehydrate, cover with water 1¹/2 inches above level of food in pot,
   boil, stir, and serve.

Black-Eyed Pea Soup

Serves 4
Weight 1 dried serving = 5.5 ounces

1. Place in a large pot:
     1 1/3 cups dried black-eyed peas, rinsed and drained
     1 whole bay leaf
     5 cups water
   Bring to a boil; then simmer, covered, for 30 minutes. Remove bay leaf.
2. Cook, then drain in a colander and set aside:
     1 cup (7 ounces) orzo (barley-shaped) pasta
3. Add to the pot of peas and simmer for 10 minutes:
     28 ounces canned crushed tomatoes
     1 onion, minced
     4 cloves garlic, minced
     1/8 teaspoon cayenne pepper
4. Stir in the cooked orzo and add:
     1/2 cup salsa
     1/2 cup red wine
     1 1/2 teaspoons salt
5. Spread on covered dehydrator trays and dehydrate for 6 hours at 145 degrees.
6. To rehydrate, cover with water 1 1/2 inches above level of food in pot, boil, stir, and serve.

Thick Vegetable Soup

Serves 4
Weight 1 dried serving = 3.5 ounces

1. Heat a Dutch oven over medium-low heat. Add:
     2 tablespoons olive oil
   When the oil is hot, add the following chopped vegetables:
     1 onion
     3 cloves garlic
     1 bell pepper
     7 medium (about 2 1/2 pounds) summer squash
       (zucchini or crookneck)
   Cook, covered, for 10 minutes, stirring occasionally.

2. Stir in:

> 15 ounces canned garbanzo beans (chickpeas), rinsed
> and drained
> 2 cups any variety stock
> 1 teaspoon honey
> 1 teaspoon wine vinegar
> 1/4 cup parsley leaves, minced

Simmer for 15 minutes.

3. Remove from heat and stir in:

> 3 cups whole-grain bread crumbs
> 1 teaspoon salt
> 3 tablespoons hot sauce
> 1/2 cup finely grated Parmesan cheese

4. Purée in a blender or food processor.
5. Spread on covered dehydrator trays and dehydrate for 6 hours at 145 degrees.
6. To rehydrate, cover with water 1 1/2 inches above level of food in pot, boil, stir, and serve.

Chowders

Tuna-Parmesan Chowder

Serves 4
Weight 1 dried serving = 4.5 ounces

This is different and delicious.

1. Heat a Dutch oven over low heat. Add:

> 2 tablespoons olive oil

When the oil is hot, add and cook for 10 minutes, stirring occasionally:

> 1 onion, minced
> 3 medium baking potatoes (about 1 1/2 pounds), scrubbed
> but not peeled, minced
> 4 stalks celery, minced
> 2 cloves garlic, minced

2. Stir in:

> 1/4 cup whole wheat flour

Add slowly, stirring:

> 1 cup any variety stock

3. Stir in and heat gently:
   1 cup milk
   13 ounces canned water-packed tuna, drained
   $^1/_4$ cup minced parsley leaves
   1 teaspoon salt
   1 teaspoon hot sauce
   Remove from heat and stir in:
   1 cup finely grated Parmesan cheese
4. Spread on covered dehydrator trays and dehydrate for 6 hours at
   145 degrees.
5. To rehydrate, cover with water $1^1/_2$ inches above level of food in pot,
   boil, stir, and serve.

Quick Clam Chowder
Serves 4
Weight 1 dried serving = 4.5 ounces

1. Heat a Dutch oven over medium-low heat. Add:
   2 tablespoons olive oil
   When the oil is hot, add and cook for 8 minutes:
   1 onion, minced
   2 cloves garlic, minced
   4 stalks celery, diced
2. Add, bring to a boil, then simmer, covered, 30 minutes longer, stirring occasionally:
   5 medium baking potatoes (about $2^1/_2$ pounds), scrubbed
       but not peeled, diced
   $19^1/_2$ ounces canned minced clams
   3 cups chicken broth, clam juice, or vegetable stock
   1 whole bay leaf
3. Remove bay leaf. Stir in:
   12 ounces canned evaporated milk
   1 teaspoon salt
   $^1/_4$ teaspoon freshly ground black pepper
4. Spread on covered dehydrator trays and dehydrate for 7 hours at
   145 degrees.
5. To rehydrate, barely cover with water. Stir while bringing to a boil;
   then serve.

*Filé powder contains
sassafras and thyme.*

Gumbo Chowder

Serves 4
Weight 1 dried serving = 4 ounces

1. Heat a Dutch oven over medium-low heat. Add:
   2 tablespoons olive oil
   When the oil is hot, add and sauté for 10 minutes:
   1 onion, chopped
   3 cloves garlic, chopped
   8 ounces stewing beef, diced, or tofu, crumbled
2. Stir in, cover, and bring to a boil:
   3 cups any variety stock
   12 ripe tomatoes (about 3 1/2 pounds), chopped
   4 ounces fresh or frozen okra, chopped
   1 cup uncooked brown rice, rinsed and drained
   2 tablespoons hot sauce
   Reduce heat and simmer for 45 minutes, or until rice is tender. Stir in:
   1 1/4 teaspoons salt
   1 teaspoon filé powder
3. Purée in a blender or food processor.
4. Spread on covered dehydrator trays and dehydrate for 6 hours at 145 degrees.
5. To rehydrate, cover with water 1 inch above level of food in pot, boil, stir, and serve.

Corn Chowder

Serves 4
Weight 1 dried serving = 3.5 ounces

This lightweight soup rehydrates into big, flavorful servings.

1. Heat in a Dutch oven over medium heat:

    3 tablespoons olive oil

    When the oil is hot, add:

    1 onion, minced

    1 carrot, grated

    3 medium baking potatoes (about 1¹/₂ pounds), diced

    Cook, stirring occasionally, for 5 minutes, or until browned.

2. Add and bring to a boil:

    3¹/₂ cups petite corn kernels, fresh, frozen, or canned

    1 bell pepper, minced

    3 cups chicken or vegetable stock

    4 cups minced cabbage (1 whole small cabbage)

    ¹/₂ teaspoon minced fresh thyme or ¹/₄ teaspoon dried thyme

    1¹/₂ teaspoons salt

    ³/₄ teaspoon freshly ground black pepper

    ¹/₈ teaspoon cayenne pepper

    Simmer for 40 minutes, or until vegetables are tender.

3. Purée in a blender or food processor.

4. Spread on covered dehydrator trays and dehydrate for 6 hours at 145 degrees.

5. To rehydrate, cover with water 1¹/₂ inches above level of food in pot, boil, stir, and serve.

Stews

New Mexican Stew

Serves 4
Weight 1 dried serving: 6 ounces

1. Heat a Dutch oven over medium-low heat. Add:

    2 tablespoons olive oil

    When the oil is hot, add and cook for 4 minutes:

    1 onion, minced

    2 medium baking potatoes (about 1 pound), peeled and grated

    Stir in and cook 3 minutes longer:

    4 cloves garlic, minced

    1 red bell pepper, minced

    1 green bell pepper, minced

2. Add and bring to a boil:

    30 ounces canned pinto beans, rinsed and drained, lightly chopped

    3 cups any variety stock

    28 ounces canned crushed tomatoes

    ³/4 cup TVP (textured vegetable protein)

    Reduce heat and simmer, covered, for 20 minutes; then remove from heat and stir in:

    ¹/2 cup red wine

    1 teaspoon salt

    ¹/2 teaspoon cayenne pepper

    1 cup grated pepper Jack cheese

3. Spread on covered dehydrator trays and dehydrate for 6¹/2 hours at 145 degrees.

4. To rehydrate, cover with water ¹/2 inch above level of food in pot, boil, stir, and serve.

Seafood Stew

1. Heat a Dutch oven over medium-low heat. Add:
   > 1 tablespoon olive oil

   When the oil is hot, add and cook for 5 minutes:
   > 1 onion, minced
   > 3 cloves garlic, minced

2. Add and bring to a boil:
   > 3 stalks celery, minced
   > 3 cups clam juice, or fish, chicken, or vegetable stock
   > 28 ounces canned crushed tomatoes
   > $1/2$ teaspoon minced fresh thyme or $1/4$ teaspoon dried thyme

3. Reduce heat; stir in and simmer 8 minutes longer, stirring occasionally:
   > 1 cup (7 ounces) orzo (barley-shaped) pasta
   > $1/2$ cup red wine
   > $1/2$ teaspoon salt
   > $1/4$ teaspoon cayenne pepper
   > 1 pound uncooked firm white boneless skinless fish fillets, such as cod, finely chopped
   > 8 ounces uncooked shrimp, shelled and deveined, finely chopped

4. Spread on covered dehydrator trays and dehydrate for 6 hours at 145 degrees.

5. To rehydrate, cover with water 2 inches above level of food in pot, boil, stir, and serve.

Chutney Lentil Stew

1. Place in a large pot:
   > $1^3/4$ cups dried lentils, rinsed and drained
   > 6 cups water
   > 1 onion, minced
   > 3 cloves garlic, minced
   > 4 stalks celery, minced

1 teaspoon fresh rosemary or ¹/₂ teaspoon dried
rosemary, minced
1 whole bay leaf
1 teaspoon olive oil

Bring to a boil; then reduce heat and simmer, covered, for 40 minutes.

2. Meanwhile, bring to a boil in a small saucepan:

1¹/₄ cups water

Add:

1 cup whole wheat couscous

Stir, cook for 15 seconds; then cover, turn off heat, and set aside.

3. Remove bay leaf from lentil mixture. Add the cooked couscous and:

³/₄ cup chutney, minced
2 teaspoons salt
¹/₄ teaspoon cayenne pepper

Blend thoroughly.

4. Spread on covered dehydrator trays and dehydrate for 6 hours at 145 degrees.

5. To rehydrate, cover with water 1¹/₂ inches above level of food in pot, boil, stir, and serve.

Fish Stew

Serves 4
Weight 1 dried serving = 4 ounces

1. Bring to a boil in a Dutch oven:

15 ounces canned chicken broth
2 cups water
28 ounces canned crushed tomatoes
8 medium baking potatoes (about 4 pounds), scrubbed
but not peeled, grated
1 bell pepper, minced
4 cloves garlic, minced
¹/₂ teaspoon minced fresh thyme or ¹/₄ teaspoon dried
thyme

Reduce heat and simmer, covered, for 40 minutes, stirring occasionally.

2. Add and simmer 5 minutes longer:

8 ounces uncooked boneless skinless fish fillets, chopped
¹/₂ cup red wine
1 teaspoon salt
¹/₄ teaspoon freshly ground black pepper
¹/₈ teaspoon cayenne pepper

3. Spread on covered dehydrator trays and dehydrate for 6¹/2 hours at 145 degrees.
4. To rehydrate, cover with water 1 inch above level of food in pot, boil, stir, and serve.

Moroccan Stew

Serves 4
Weight 1 dried serving = 4 ounces

---

1. Heat a Dutch oven over medium-low heat. Add:
   > **2 tablespoons olive oil**
   When the oil is hot, add and cook for 3 minutes:
   > **1 onion, minced**
   > **3 cloves garlic, minced**
   Add and cook 5 minutes longer:
   > **2 carrots, grated**
   > **1 bell pepper, minced**
   > **10 fresh mushrooms, minced**
2. Add and bring to a boil:
   > **4 cups any variety stock**
   > **4¹/4 ounces canned chopped ripe (black) olives**
   > **15 ounces canned small white beans, rinsed and drained**
   > **juice of 1 lemon (2 tablespoons juice)**
   > **1 teaspoon honey**
   > **1 teaspoon salt**
   > **¹/2 teaspoon crushed dried oregano**
   > **¹/2 teaspoon crushed red pepper flakes**
   > **¹/2 teaspoon freshly ground black pepper**
   Reduce heat and simmer for 5 minutes.
3. Stir in:
   > **³/4 cup whole wheat couscous**
   Cover and cook 3 minutes longer.
4. Spread on covered dehydrator trays and dehydrate for 6 hours at 145 degrees.
5. To rehydrate, cover with water 1¹/2 inches above level of food in pot, boil, stir, and serve.

Black Bean Stew

Serves 4
Weight 1 dried serving = 4.5 ounces

1. Cook, then drain in a colander and set aside:
   1 cup (8 ounces) riso (rice-shaped) pasta
2. Place in the pot:
   45 ounces canned black beans, rinsed and drained
   3 cups any variety stock
   3 scallions, minced
   3 cloves garlic, minced
   4 ounces canned diced green chilies
   1 teaspoon salt
   1 teaspoon olive oil
   3 tablespoons hot sauce
   1 tablespoon Worcestershire sauce
   Bring to a boil, then remove from heat. Stir in the cooked pasta.
3. Spread on covered dehydrator trays and dehydrate for 5 hours at 145 degrees.
4. To rehydrate, cover with water 1¹/₂ inches above level of food in pot, boil, stir, and serve.

Vegetable Stew

Serves 4
Weight 1 dried serving = 4.5 ounces

1. Heat a Dutch oven over medium heat. Add:
   1 tablespoon olive oil
   When the oil is hot, add:
   1 large onion, minced
   3 cloves garlic, minced
   ¹/₂ teaspoon ground cumin
   Cook for 5 minutes, stirring occasionally.

Simmer the stew with wine and garlic.

2. Add:

> 4 medium baking potatoes (about 2 pounds), peeled and diced
> 10 fresh mushrooms, diced
> 3 cups any variety stock or water
> $^1/_2$ cup red wine
> 28 ounces canned crushed tomatoes
> 1 cup dried lentils, rinsed and drained
> 2 tablespoons minced fresh basil or 1 tablespoon dried basil
> 1 teaspoon salt
> $^1/_2$ teaspoon crushed red pepper flakes

Bring to a boil; then reduce heat to very low and simmer, covered, stirring occasionally, for $1^1/_2$ hours, or until lentils and potatoes are tender.

3. Spread on covered dehydrator trays and dehydrate for $6^1/_2$ hours at 145 degrees.
4. To rehydrate, cover with water $1^1/_2$ inches above level of food in pot, boil, stir, and serve.

Quick Beef Stew

Serves 4
Weight 1 dried serving = 4.5 ounces

1. Heat a Dutch oven over medium heat. Add:

> 1 tablespoon olive oil

When the oil is hot, add and cook, stirring, for 4 minutes, or until light brown:

> 1 pound lean ground round or ground turkey
> 1 onion, minced
> 1 carrot, grated

2. Add and bring to a boil:

> 3 cups any variety stock
> 28 ounces canned crushed tomatoes
> 1 whole bay leaf
> 1 teaspoon minced fresh thyme or $^1/_2$ teaspoon dried thyme
> 1 teaspoon salt
> 1 teaspoon chili powder

15 ounces canned small white beans, rinsed and drained

3/4 cup whole wheat couscous

Reduce heat and simmer, covered, for 12 minutes.

3. Spread on covered dehydrator trays and dehydrate for 5 1/2 hours at 145 degrees.

4. To rehydrate, cover with water 1 inch above level of food in pot, boil, stir, and serve.

North African Stew

Serves 4
Weight 1 dried serving = 4 ounces

This dish combines well-browned roasted vegetables with whole wheat couscous.

1. Preheat oven to 450 degrees.

2. Mix together in a 10-by-13-inch glass casserole dish:

1 large eggplant, diced

2 carrots, grated

2 large onions, diced

Add and mix well:

1 tablespoon olive oil

Bake for 45 minutes, stirring occasionally.

3. Add to the mixture and blend well:

28 ounces canned crushed tomatoes

15 ounces canned small white beans, rinsed and drained

3 cups water

3/4 cups whole wheat couscous

1/2 teaspoon salt

1/2 teaspoon freshly ground black pepper

1/4 teaspoon ground cinnamon

2 teaspoons minced fresh mint or 1 teaspoon dried mint

4. Return the stew to the oven and bake for 10 minutes. Stir and return to the oven for 10 minutes longer. Remove from oven and let stand for 15 minutes.

5. Spread on covered dehydrator trays and dehydrate for 6 hours at 145 degrees.

6. To rehydrate, cover with water 1 inch above level of food in pot, boil, stir, and serve.

Hot Dog Stew

Serves 4
Weight 1 dried serving = 5 ounces

1. Bring to a rolling boil in a large pot:
    8 cups any variety stock or water
    Stir in:
    8 ounces farfalline (tiny bow) pasta
    Return to a boil; then add:
    3 beef, pork, turkey, or soy hot dogs, finely chopped
    1 bell pepper, minced
    Cook for 7 minutes, or until pasta is tender. *Do not drain.*
2. Stir in:
    3 cups spaghetti sauce
    $^1/_4$ teaspoon cayenne pepper
3. Remove from heat and stir in:
    $^1/_2$ cup finely grated Parmesan cheese
4. Spread on covered dehydrator trays and dehydrate for 6 hours at 145 degrees.
5. To rehydrate, cover with water just above level of food in pot, boil, stir, and serve.

Chilies, Beans, and Pilaf

Southwestern Chili

Serves 4
Weight 1 dried serving = 5 ounces

1. Heat a Dutch oven over medium-low heat; then add:
    2 tablespoons olive oil
    When the oil is hot, add and cook for 5 minutes:
    2 onions, finely chopped
    4 cloves garlic, minced
2. Add and stir for 2 minutes:
    1 tablespoon ground cumin
    $^1/_2$ teaspoon ground cloves
3. Add:
    3 cups water
    30 ounces canned pinto beans, rinsed and drained
    28 ounces canned crushed tomatoes

1¹/₂ cups TVP (textured vegetable protein)
2 tablespoons chili powder
1 tablespoon hot sauce
1 teaspoon salt
1 teaspoon honey

Bring to a boil; then reduce heat and simmer for 10 minutes.

4. Spread on covered dehydrator trays and dehydrate for 6 hours at 145 degrees.
5. To rehydrate, cover with water 1¹/₂ inches above level of food in pot, boil, stir, and serve.

Turkey Chili
Serves 4
Weight 1 dried serving = 4 ounces

---

1. Heat a Dutch oven over medium heat. Add:
   1 tablespoon olive oil
   When the oil is hot, add and cook, stirring, for 5 minutes:
   1 onion, minced
   1 bell pepper, minced
   2 cloves garlic, minced
2. Add and stir 3 minutes longer:
   1 pound uncooked ground turkey or diced roasted turkey
   1 tablespoon chili powder
   1 teaspoon ground cumin
3. Stir in and bring to a boil:
   28 ounces canned crushed tomatoes
   3 cups any variety stock or water
   ¹/₂ cup whole wheat couscous
   ¹/₂ teaspoon salt
   ¹/₄ teaspoon cayenne pepper
   Reduce heat and simmer, covered, for 10 minutes.
4. Remove from heat and stir in:
   ¹/₂ cup finely grated Parmesan or Romano cheese
5. Spread on covered dehydrator trays and dehydrate for 6 hours at 145 degrees.
6. To rehydrate, cover with water 1¹/₂ inches above level of food in pot, boil, stir, and serve.

Canyon Country Chili

Serves 4
Weight 1 dried serving = 5 ounces

1. Heat a Dutch oven over medium heat. Add:

   1 tablespoon olive oil

   When the oil is hot, add and cook for 3 minutes:

   3 leeks (white parts only) or 1 onion, minced
   2 cloves garlic, minced
   1 bell pepper, minced

2. Stir in and cook 3 minutes longer:

   1 teaspoon chili powder
   1 teaspoon salt
   $^1/_4$ teaspoon curry powder
   $^1/_4$ teaspoon crushed red pepper flakes

3. Add and bring to a boil:

   15 ounces canned black beans, rinsed and drained
   28 ounces canned crushed tomatoes
   2 cups any variety stock or water
   1$^1/_4$ cups whole wheat couscous

   Reduce heat to low and add:

   6 ounces soy ground round, crumbled
   $^1/_4$ cup red wine

   Simmer for 3 minutes.

4. Spread on covered dehydrator trays and dehydrate for 6 hours at 145 degrees.

5. To rehydrate, cover with water 1$^1/_2$ inches above level of food in pot, boil, stir, and serve.

Bacon Baked Beans

Serves 4
Weight 1 dried serving = 4.5 ounces

Use your choice of pork or soy bacon.

1. Heat a Dutch oven over medium heat. Add:

   1 tablespoon olive oil

   When the oil is hot, add and cook for 8 minutes, stirring occasionally:

   2 onions, minced

2. Add and bring to a boil, then reduce heat and simmer for 5 minutes:

   28 ounces canned baked beans
   28 ounces canned crushed tomatoes
   $^1/_2$ cup water

$^1/_2$ cup dried bacon chips (pork or soy)
1 teaspoon honey or sugar
1 teaspoon cider vinegar
1 teaspoon liquid smoke

3. Spread on covered dehydrator trays and dehydrate for 6 hours at 145 degrees.
4. To rehydrate, cover with water $1^1/_2$ inches above level of food in pot, boil, stir, and serve.

Fiesta Frijoles

Serves 4
Weight 1 dried serving = 4.5 ounces

1. Cook and drain in a colander, reserving the liquid:
     $5^3/_4$ cups cooked beans
2. Heat a Dutch oven or large skillet over medium heat. Add:
     2 tablespoons canola oil
   When the oil is hot, add:
     1 onion, minced
     3 cloves garlic, minced
     1 bell pepper, minced
     1 tablespoon chili powder
     1 teaspoon ground cumin
   Cook for 5 minutes, stirring occasionally.
3. Coarsely chop $5^3/_4$ cups of cooked beans and $1^1/_4$ cups of the bean liquid in a blender or food processor. Add the beans to the onion mixture, along with:
     2 cups chopped tomatoes, fresh or canned
     4 ounces canned diced green chilies
     $1^1/_2$ teaspoons salt
   Simmer for 5 minutes.
4. Remove from heat and stir in:
     1 cup grated Monterey Jack, hoop, or other mild white cheese
5. Spread on covered dehydrator trays and dehydrate for 6 hours at 145 degrees.
6. To rehydrate, cover with water 1 inch above level of food in pot. Stir while bringing to a boil, and then serve.

Chicken Pilaf

1. Toast in a small skillet over medium heat until lightly browned:

   2 cups uncooked kasha (buckwheat groats)

   Set aside.

2. Heat a Dutch oven over medium heat. Add:

   2 tablespoons olive oil

   When the oil is hot, add and cook, stirring, for 5 minutes:

   1 onion, minced

   3 cloves garlic, minced

   2 carrots, grated

   2 bell peppers, diced

   2 uncooked boneless skinless chicken breast fillets
      (12 ounces total), diced

3. Add the kasha and:

   $^1/_2$ cup chopped almonds

   1 $^1/_2$ teaspoons salt

   $^1/_2$ teaspooon cinnamon

   $^1/_2$ teaspoon cayenne pepper

   3 cups any variety stock

   3 cups spaghetti sauce

   Bring to a boil; then reduce heat to very low and simmer, stirring occasionally, for 15 minutes, or until kasha is tender.

4. Spread on covered dehydrator trays and dehydrate for 6 hours at 145 degrees.

5. To rehydrate, cover with water 1$^1/_2$ inches above level of food in pot, boil, stir, and serve.

CHAPTER FIVE

PASTA DISHES AND CASSEROLES

Pasta is every backpacker's first choice for a tasty, filling dinner. Fortunately, it's easy to dehydrate your favorite spaghetti dinner or combination dishes such as chow mein, curry, or even lasagna, to enjoy while backpacking. Casseroles of all sorts can be dried and rehydrated instantly in camp by barely covering them with water, bringing to a boil, stirring, and serving. Why should backpackers dry grains, such as rice, kasha, bulgur, and pasta? These uncooked grains are heavy and bulky. They take both time and fuel to cook in the field. Instead, completely cook them, incorporating the grains into a complete meal; then dry the meal at home. The pasta and grains will be far lighter in weight, more compact, and will reheat much faster. No cooking, no sticky pots, just heating in the field.

About Pasta

So many choices: corn, soy, buckwheat, semolina, whole wheat, and more. All types of pasta dehydrate well. Before cooking your pasta, break the strands of long pasta, such as spaghetti, linguini, or vermicelli, into thirds. Your dish will cook and dry faster, and the dehydrated pasta will pack more easily into small plastic bags for backpacking. At home, bring a pot of water to a full rolling boil. Toss in the strands of

pasta and add a drop of oil; this will keep the strands from sticking together. Cook your pasta just long enough—al dente—as though you were preparing it for tonight's dinner. Al dente pasta will remain so after dehydrating it and rehydrating it in the field.

When my Italian friend Rachele cooks pasta, she stands over the pot, watching it carefully and stirring it gently once a minute. As soon as it is done—each strand soft outside but still slightly chewy inside—she turns off the heat and drains and serves the pasta. Is it worth such careful attention? Yes, it is; Rachele's perfectly cooked pasta brings tears to your eyes when you taste it.

Meatless Pasta Dishes

Sierra Spaghetti
Serves 4
Weight 1 dried serving = 6 ounces

This is high in protein and full of flavor.

1. Heat a Dutch oven or large skillet over medium heat. Add:
   2 tablespoons olive oil
   When the oil is hot, add and sauté for 10 minutes:
   1 onion, diced
   10 fresh mushrooms, diced
   4 cloves garlic, minced
2. Add and cook for 5 minutes, stirring occasionally:
   3¹/₂ cups spaghetti sauce
   4¹/₂ ounces canned chopped ripe (black) olives
   15 ounces canned small white beans, rinsed and drained
   1 teaspoon crushed red pepper flakes
   ¹/₂ teaspoon dried oregano
3. Cook, then drain in a colander:
   12 ounces linguini pasta, broken in thirds
   Place pasta back in pot. Add the sauce and stir well.
4. Spread on covered dehydrator trays and dehydrate for 6 hours at 145 degrees.
5. To rehydrate, cover with water ¹/₂ inch above level of food in pot, boil, stir, and serve.

Tomato Pasta Pesto

This is filling and flavorful.

1. Purée in a blender or food processor until smooth:
    1/2 cup finely grated Parmesan cheese
    5 cloves garlic
    1 bunch fresh basil leaves
    1 teaspoon salt
    1/4 cup olive oil
2. Cook, then drain in a colander:
    16 ounces linguini pasta, broken in thirds
3. Toss the pasta with the sauce. Stir in:
    3 cups spaghetti sauce
4. Spread on covered dehydrator trays and dehydrate for 6 hours at 145 degrees.
5. To rehydrate, cover with water 1/2 inch above level of food in pot, boil, stir, and serve.

Stu's Zippy Spaghetti

1. Cook, then drain in a colander:
    14 ounces whole wheat spaghetti, broken in thirds
    Set aside.
2. Heat a large skillet over medium-low heat. Add:
    2 tablespoons olive oil
    When the oil is hot, add and sauté for 8 minutes:
    1 onion, minced
    2 cloves garlic, minced
    1 bell pepper, minced
    1 carrot, grated
    10 fresh mushrooms, minced
3. Stir in and cook 5 minutes longer:
    28 ounces canned crushed tomatoes
    1/2 cup water
    1/2 cup salsa, mild, medium, or hot
    1/2 cup TVP (textured vegetable protein)
    1/2 teaspoon salt

4. Remove from heat and stir in:
       ¹/2 cup finely grated Romano cheese
   Mix sauce with pasta, stirring to coat.
5. Spread on covered dehydrator trays and dehydrate for 6 hours at 145 degrees.
6. To rehydrate, cover with water ¹/2 inch above level of food in pot, boil, stir, and serve.

Tofu Tetrazzini

Serves 4
Weight 1 dried serving = 5.5 ounces

This is delicious.
1. Cook, then drain in a colander:
       12 ounces (3¹/2 cups) small shell pasta
   Set aside.
2. Heat a large skillet or Dutch oven over medium-low heat. Add:
       3 tablespoons olive oil
   When the oil is hot, add and sauté for 5 minutes:
       1 onion, minced
       10 fresh mushrooms, minced
       ¹/4 cup finely chopped almonds
   Add:
       ¹/4 cup whole wheat flour
   Cook, stirring, for 3 minutes.
3. Stir in and cook 3 minutes longer:
       8 ounces firm tofu, drained and crumbled
       2 cups plain yogurt
       ¹/4 cup dry white wine
       ³/4 teaspoon salt
       ¹/4 teaspoon cayenne pepper
4. Remove from heat and stir in:
       ¹/2 cup finely grated Parmesan cheese
   Add the sauce to the cooked pasta.
5. Spread on covered dehydrator trays and dehydrate for 6 hours at 145 degrees.
6. To rehydrate, cover with water ¹/2 inch above level of food in pot, boil, stir, and serve.

Sweet and Sour Noodles

Serves 4
Weight 1 dried serving = 5.5 ounces

This dish has a piquant ginger and pineapple flavor.

1. Cook, then drain in a colander:

    14 ounces vermicelli pasta, broken in thirds

    Return the pasta to the cooking pot and set aside.

2. Heat a large skillet over medium-low heat. Add:

    1 tablespoon sesame oil

    When the oil is hot, add and stir for 2 minutes:

    3 cloves garlic, minced

    3 tablespoons minced fresh ginger root

    1 onion, minced

3. Reduce heat to low; add and cook for 5 minutes:

    4 whole ripe tomatoes, diced

    1 green bell pepper, minced

    20 ounces canned crushed pineapple with juice

    $^1/_2$ cup TVP (textured vegetable protein)

    3 tablespoons rice or cider vinegar

    2 tablespoons brown sugar

    2 tablespoons tamari soy sauce

    $^1/_2$ teaspoon salt

4. Mix together in a small bowl:

    1 tablespoon cornstarch mixed with 3 tablespoons cold water

    Add the cornstarch to the skillet and cook 1 minute longer.

5. Stir the sauce and pasta in the pot.

6. Spread on covered dehydrator trays and dehydrate for 6 hours at 145 degrees.

7. To rehydrate, cover with water $^1/_2$ inch above level of food in pot, boil, stir, and serve.

Falafel Spaghetti

Serves 4
Weight 1 dried serving = 7.5 ounces

1. Mix together in a small bowl:
   2 cups dried falafel mix
   ³/4 cup water
   Let stand for 5 minutes; then roll into 28 balls the size of walnuts.
   Flatten them slightly.
2. Heat a large skillet over medium-low heat. Add:
   2 tablespoons olive oil
   Fry the falafel balls until evenly browned on all sides; then pour over
   them:
   ¹/2 cup water
   Reduce heat to very low, cover, and cook for 5 minutes.
3. Cook, then drain in a colander:
   ¹/4 ounce thin spaghetti, broken in thirds
4. Mix together the spaghetti, falafel balls, and:
   3¹/2 cups spaghetti sauce
5. Spread on covered dehydrator trays, crumbling the falafel balls, and
   dehydrate for 4¹/2 hours at 145 degrees.
6. To rehydrate, cover with water ¹/2 inch above level of food in pot,
   boil, stir, and serve.

Sesame Pasta

Serves 4
Weight 1 dried serving = 7 ounces

1. Purée in a blender or food processor:
   3 cloves garlic
   ¹/4 cup olive oil
   ¹/2 cup water
   ³/4 cup TVP (textured vegetable protein)
   1¹/4 cups sesame seeds
   juice of 1 fresh lemon (2 tablespoons juice)
   2 tablespoons honey
   1¹/4 teaspoons salt
   1 teaspoon crushed red pepper flakes
2. Cook, then drain in a colander:
   16 ounces vermicelli pasta, broken in thirds
3. Toss the sauce with the pasta, stirring well to coat.

4. Spread on covered dehydrator trays and dehydrate for 4 hours at 145 degrees.
5. To rehydrate, cover with water just above level of food in pot, boil, stir, and serve.

Pan-Fried Whole-Grain Noodles

Serves 4
Weight 1 dried serving = 5.5 ounces

This is a favorite dish.
1. Cook, then drain thoroughly in a colander:
    1 pound buckwheat or whole wheat spaghetti
2. Heat a Dutch oven over medium-low heat. Add:
    2 tablespoons sesame oil
   When the oil is hot, add and cook for 5 minutes:
    1 onion, minced
    1 carrot, grated
    3 cloves garlic, minced
3. Add the cooked, drained pasta. Cook, stirring occasionally, for 5 minutes, or until brown.
4. Stir in:
    2 tablespoons tamari soy sauce
    ¹/₂ cup finely chopped cashews
   Cook for a minute, then add:
    6 eggs, beaten
    1 teaspoon salt
    ¹/₂ teaspoon crushed red pepper flakes
   Cook for 5 minutes, or until eggs are set.
5. Spread on covered dehydrator trays and dehydrate for 4 hours at 145 degrees.
6. To rehydrate, cover with water just above level of food in pot, boil, stir, and serve.

Use sesame oil and cashews.

Teriyaki Noodles

Serves 4
Weight 1 dried serving = 6.5 ounces

1. Cook, then drain in a colander:
       14 ounces linguini pasta, broken in thirds
   Replace pasta in pot and set aside.
2. Heat a large skillet over medium-low heat. Add:
       3 tablespoons olive oil
   When the oil is hot, add and sauté for 5 minutes:
       1 onion, minced
       3 cloves garlic, minced
   Add:
       $1/4$ cup whole wheat flour
       1 tablespoon minced fresh ginger
   Cook, stirring, for 3 minutes.
3. Stir in slowly:
       1 cup any variety stock
4. Stir in and cook 5 minutes longer:
       1 pound firm tofu, drained and crumbled
       $1/4$ cup TVP (textured vegetable protein)
       3 tablespoons tamari soy sauce
       3 tablespoons honey
       $1/2$ teaspoon salt
5. Mix sauce with pasta.
6. Spread on covered dehydrator trays and dehydrate for $5^1/2$ hours at 145 degrees.
7. To rehydrate, cover with water just above level of food in pot, boil, stir, and serve.

Thai Noodles

Serves 4
Weight 1 dried serving = 6 ounces

This spicy peanut sauce will wake up your taste buds.
1. Cook, then drain in a colander:
       18 ounces vermicelli pasta, broken in thirds
   Set aside.
2. Heat a Dutch oven over medium-low heat. Add:
       1 tablespoon sesame oil

When the oil is hot, add and sauté for 2 minutes:

    10 mushrooms, minced

    5 cloves garlic, minced

    3 shallots or scallions, minced

3. Reduce heat to low. Add the cooked, drained noodles and:

    $3/4$ cup dry-roasted peanuts, finely chopped

    2 tablespoons minced fresh ginger

    4 tablespoons tamari soy sauce

    1 teaspoon salt

    $3/4$ teaspoon crushed red pepper flakes

Cook, stirring occasionally, for 8 minutes.

4. Spread on covered dehydrator trays and dehydrate for 4 hours at 145 degrees.

5. To rehydrate, cover with water just above level of food in pot, boil, stir, and serve.

Creamy Pasta

Serves 4
Weight 1 dried serving = 5.5 ounces

1. Cook, then drain in a colander:

    10 ounces capellini pasta

Return pasta to pot and set aside.

2. Heat a large skillet over medium-low heat. Add:

    1 tablespoon olive oil

When the oil is hot, add and cook for 8 minutes, stirring occasionally:

    4 cloves garlic, minced

    1 onion, minced

    5 fresh mushrooms, minced

Add and cook 5 minutes longer:

    15 ounces canned pumpkin purée

    15 ounces canned small white beans, rinsed and drained

    $1/2$ teaspoon salt

    $1/2$ teaspoon freshly ground black pepper

    $1/4$ teaspoon ground nutmeg

    $1/8$ teaspoon cayenne pepper

Remove from heat and stir in:

    10 ounces chèvre (goat cheese), crumbled

3. Add the sauce to the pasta in the pot. Stir to blend.
4. Spread on covered dehydrator trays and dehydrate for 6 hours at 145 degrees.
5. To rehydrate, cover with water barely above level of food in pot, boil, stir, and serve.

Portobello Curry
Serves 4
Weight 1 dried serving = 6 ounces

---

1. Heat a Dutch oven or large skillet over medium heat. Add:
   2 tablespoons olive oil
   When the oil is hot, add and sauté for 10 minutes:
   1 onion, minced
   2 whole portobello mushrooms (1 pound), minced
   4 cloves garlic, minced
2. Add and cook, stirring occasionally, for 2 minutes:
   1 tablespoon whole wheat flour
   1 tablespoon curry powder
3. Add and bring to a boil:
   15 ounces canned small white beans, rinsed and drained
   1 cup any variety stock
4. Stir in:
   2 cups plain yogurt
   1 teaspoon salt
   $^{1}/_{2}$ teaspoon crushed red pepper flakes
   Set aside.
5. Cook, then drain in a colander:
   12 ounces thin spaghetti, broken in thirds
   Return the pasta to the pot. Add the sauce and blend well.
6. Spread on covered dehydrator trays and dehydrate for 6 hours at 145 degrees.
7. To rehydrate, cover with water just above level of food in pot, boil, stir, and serve.

Pasta Genovese

This pasta features a walnut sauce.

1. Purée in a blender or food processor until smooth:

   5 cloves garlic, minced
   1 bunch fresh parsley leaves
   1 bunch fresh basil leaves
   1^1/$_2$ cups shelled walnuts
   ^{1}/$_4$ cup olive oil
   ^{1}/$_2$ cup finely grated Parmesan cheese
   ^{1}/$_2$ cup water
   1 teaspoon salt

2. Cook:

   18 ounces capellini pasta, broken in thirds

   During the last 3 minutes of cooking, stir in:

   ^{1}/$_3$ cup TVP (textured vegetable protein)

   Drain in a colander; then return to pot.

3. Stir the nut sauce into the pasta, blending well.
4. Spread on covered dehydrator trays and dehydrate for 5^1/$_2$ hours at 145 degrees.
5. To rehydrate, barely cover with water above level of food in pot. Bring to a boil, stirring, and serve.

Linguini with Mushroom Sauce

1. Cook, then drain in a colander:

   1 pound linguini pasta

   Return the pasta to the pot and set aside.

2. Heat a large skillet over medium heat. Add:

   2 tablespoons olive oil

   When the oil is hot, add and stir for 8 minutes:

   1 onion, minced
   3 cloves garlic, minced
   9 mushrooms, minced

3. Add and cook 3 minutes longer:
   > **¹/₄ cup whole wheat flour**

   Stir in slowly:
   > **3 cups milk**
   > **15 ounces canned small white beans, rinsed and drained**

4. Remove from heat and stir in:
   > **¹/₄ cup white wine**
   > **¹/₂ cup finely grated Parmesan cheese**

5. Mix the sauce with the pasta.
6. Spread on covered dehydrator trays and dehydrate for 6 hours at 145 degrees.
7. To rehydrate, cover with water just above level of food in pot, boil, stir, and serve.

Gruyère Pasta
Serves 4
Weight 1 dried serving = 6.5 ounces

1. Cook, then drain in a colander:
   > **12 ounces vermicelli pasta, broken in thirds**

   Replace pasta in pot and set aside.

2. Heat a large skillet over low heat. Add:
   > **2 tablespoons olive oil**

   When the oil is hot, add and cook, stirring, for 3 minutes:
   > **4 cloves garlic, minced**
   > **¹/₂ cup whole wheat flour**
   > **2 tablespoons fresh basil, minced, or 1 tablespoon dried basil**

3. Add slowly, stirring constantly:
   > **2 cups any variety stock, milk, or water**

4. Reduce heat, stir in, and cook for 2 minutes:
   > **15 ounces canned small white beans, rinsed and drained**
   > **¹/₂ cup TVP (textured vegetable protein)**
   > **¹/₂ cup dry white wine**
   > **³/₄ teaspoon salt**
   > **¹/₄ teaspoon ground white pepper**
   > **¹/₈ teaspoon ground nutmeg**

   Remove from heat and stir in:
   > **4 ounces Gruyère cheese (1 cup chopped)**

5. Add the sauce to the pasta in the pot, stirring well to coat.
6. Spread on covered dehydrator trays and dehydrate for 5 hours at 145 degrees.
7. To rehydrate, cover with water barely above level of food in pot, boil, stir, and serve.

Pasta with Meat or Seafood

Spicy Chicken

Serves 4
Weight 1 dried serving = 6.5 ounces

1. Cook, then drain in a colander:
      1 pound vermicelli pasta, broken in thirds
   Return pasta to the pot and set aside.
2. Heat a large skillet over medium-low heat. Add:
      1 tablespoon olive oil
   When the oil is hot, add and stir for 3 minutes:
      1 onion, minced
      2 cloves garlic, minced
      2 uncooked skinless boneless chicken breast fillets
         (12 ounces total), minced
3. Add:
      28 ounces canned crushed tomatoes
      4 ounces canned diced green chilies
      1 tablespoon chili powder
      $1/2$ teaspoon salt
      $1/4$ teaspoon cayenne pepper
   Bring to a boil; then reduce heat and simmer for 10 minutes.
4. Remove from heat and stir in:
      1 cup any variety grated cheese
5. Toss the chicken mixture with the cooked pasta.
6. Spread on covered dehydrator trays and dehydrate for 6 hours at 145 degrees.
7. To rehydrate, cover with water just above level of food in pot. Stir while bringing to a boil, and then serve.

Shrimp Whimsy

Serves 4
Weight 1 dried serving = 4.5 ounces

1. Cook, then drain in a colander:
   14 ounces capellini pasta
   Return the pasta to the pot and set aside.
2. Heat a large skillet over medium-low heat. Add:
   1 tablespoon sesame oil
   When the oil is hot, add and sauté for 1 minute:
   3 cloves garlic, minced
   3 scallions, minced
3. Add:

   28 ounces canned crushed tomatoes
   8 ounces uncooked shrimp, shelled and deveined, finely chopped
   10 edible-podded (sugar or snap) peas, diced
   20 ounces canned crushed pineapple
   1 tablespoon minced fresh ginger
   $1/2$ teaspoon salt
   $1/4$ teaspoon cayenne pepper
   Bring to a boil; then reduce heat and simmer for 3 minutes.
4. Add the sauce to the pasta in the pot and stir.
5. Spread on covered dehydrator trays and dehydrate for 6 hours at 145 degrees.
6. To rehydrate, cover with water just above level of food in pot, boil, stir, and serve.

Clam Vermicelli

Serves 4
Weight 1 dried serving = 6 ounces

1. Cook, then drain in a colander:
   14 ounces vermicelli pasta, broken in thirds
   Return the pasta to the pot and set aside.
2. Heat a large skillet or Dutch oven over medium-low heat. Add:
   1 tablespoon olive oil
   When the oil is hot, add and sauté for 3 minutes:
   4 cloves garlic, minced
   Add and cook for 5 minutes:
   10 fresh mushrooms, minced

3. Add and cook 5 minutes longer:
> **28 ounces canned crushed tomatoes**
> **^{1}/4 cup minced fresh basil or parsley leaves**
> **^{1}/2 teaspoon crushed red pepper flakes**
> **^{1}/2 teaspoon salt**

Stir in:
> **12 ounces canned minced clams, drained**

4. Remove from heat and stir in:
> **^{1}/2 cup finely grated Parmesan cheese**
5. Toss the sauce with the pasta.
6. Spread on covered dehydrator trays and dehydrate for 6 hours at 145 degrees.
7. To rehydrate, cover with water ^{1}/2 inch above level of food in pot, boil, stir, and serve.

Seafood Newburg

Serves 4
Weight 1 dried serving = 6 ounces

---

1. Cook, then drain in a colander:
> **1^3/4 cups (14 ounces) riso (rice-shaped) pasta**

Return the pasta to the pot and set aside.
2. Melt in the top of a double boiler:
> **^{1}/4 cup butter or margarine**

Add, stirring constantly:
> **^{1}/2 cup whole wheat flour**
3. Add gradually, stirring until thickened:
> **2^1/2 cups milk or cream**
4. Stir in and cook for 5 minutes:
> **2^1/2 cups (about 1 pound) cooked, diced lobster, crab, shrimp, or boneless fish**
> **^{1}/4 cup dry sherry**
> **^{1}/2 teaspoon salt**
> **^{1}/8 teaspoon cayenne pepper**
> **^{1}/8 teaspoon ground nutmeg**
5. Stir the sauce and the pasta.
6. Spread on covered dehydrator trays and dehydrate for 6 hours at 145 degrees.
7. To rehydrate, cover with water ^{1}/2 inch above level of food in pot, boil, stir, and serve.

Saucy Tuna

Serves 4
Weight 1 dried serving = 6 ounces

This is very easy to make and very tasty.
1. Cook, then drain in a colander:
   12 ounces vermicelli pasta, broken in thirds
   Return the pasta to the pot and set aside.
2. Heat a large skillet over medium-low heat; then add:
   2 tablespoons olive oil
   When the oil is hot, add and cook, stirring, for 5 minutes:
   1 onion, minced
   4 cloves garlic, minced
   Add and cook 3 minutes longer:
   28 ounces canned crushed tomatoes
   4 ounces canned diced green chilies
   12 ounces water-packed canned tuna, drained
   $^1/_2$ teaspoon salt
3. Stir together the drained pasta and sauce. Stir in:
   $^1/_3$ cup finely grated Parmesan cheese.
4. Spread on covered dehydrator trays and dehydrate for $5^1/_2$ hours at 145 degrees.
5. To rehydrate, cover with water $^1/_2$ inch above level of food in pot, boil, stir, and serve.

Shrimp Capellini

Serves 4
Weight 1 dried serving = 5.5 ounces

1. Cook, then drain in a colander:
   14 ounces capellini pasta
   Set aside.
2. Heat a large skillet or Dutch oven over medium-low heat. Add:
   1 tablespoon olive oil
   When the oil is hot, add and sauté for 3 minutes:
   1 onion, minced
   Add and cook for 5 more minutes:
   6 fresh mushrooms, minced
   $^1/_2$ teaspoon minced fresh rosemary or $^1/_4$ teaspoon dried rosemary

3. Add and cook 5 minutes longer:
   28 ounces canned crushed tomatoes
   8 ounces uncooked shelled, deveined shrimp, finely
      chopped
   $1/2$ cup red wine
   $1/2$ teaspoon salt
   $1/8$ teaspoon cayenne pepper
4. Combine sauce and pasta, stirring to blend well.
5. Spread on covered dehydrator trays and dehydrate for 6 hours at
   145 degrees.
6. To rehydrate, cover with water 1 inch above level of food in pot,
   boil, stir, and serve.

Crab Fettucini with Parsley-Mint Sauce

Serves 4
Weight 1 dried serving = 5 ounces

1. Cook, then drain in a colander:
   12 ounces fettucini pasta, broken in thirds
   Replace pasta in pot and set aside.
2. Heat a large skillet over medium-low heat. Add:
   1 tablespoon olive oil
   When the oil is hot, add and sauté for 1 minute:
   4 cloves garlic, minced
   Add and stir for a few minutes:
   28 ounces canned crushed tomatoes
   1 pound raw or cooked crab meat or imitation crab,
      flaked
   juice of 1 fresh lemon (2 tablespoons juice)
   $1/2$ teaspoon salt
   $1/4$ teaspoon cayenne pepper
   $1/2$ cup minced fresh parsley leaves
   1 tablespooon minced fresh mint leaves or 1 teaspoon
      dried mint
3. Add the sauce to the cooked, drained pasta, stirring to blend well.
4. Spread on covered dehydrator trays and dehydrate for 5 hours at
   145 degrees.
5. To rehydrate, cover with water $1/2$ inch above level of food in pot,
   boil, stir, and serve.

Tandoori Fish

Serves 4
Weight 1 dried serving = 5 ounces

1. Cook, then drain in a colander:
      3 cups (20 ounces) orzo (barley-shaped) pasta
   Oil a 10-by-13-inch casserole dish. Spread the cooked, drained pasta in the dish.
2. Cover the pasta with:
      1 pound uncooked boneless skinless fish fillets, diced
3. Preheat oven to 350 degrees.
4. Blend together in a blender or food processor:
      1 small onion, minced
      5 cloves garlic, minced
      3 cups plain yogurt
      juice of 1 fresh lemon (2 tablespoons juice)
      1 tablespoon ground ginger
      1 tablespoon chili powder
      1 tablespoon ground turmeric
      1 tablespoon ground cumin
      1¹/₂ teaspoons salt
5. Pour the yogurt mixture over the fish and pasta. Bake for 20 minutes.
6. Spread on covered dehydrator trays, flaking the fish, and dehydrate for 6 hours at 145 degrees.
7. To rehydrate, cover with water 1 inch above level of food in pot, boil, stir, and serve.

Fresh lemon juice compliments fresh fish.

Cowboy Pasta

Serves 4
Weight 1 dried serving = 5.5 ounces

1. Cook, then drain in a colander:
   10 ounces (2¹/₂ cups) farfalline (tiny bow) pasta
   Return pasta to pot and set aside.
2. Sauté until browned in a large nonstick skillet over medium heat:
   8 ounces lean ground beef or turkey
   or use 6 ounces soy ground round, crumbled (add after
   salsa; no sautéing is needed)
3. Add to the skillet and bring to a boil:
   28 ounces canned crushed tomatoes
   15 ounces canned "ranch style" beans
   ¹/₃ cup salsa, mild, medium, or hot
   Simmer for 4 minutes.
4. Remove from heat and stir in:
   ³/₄ cup finely grated Parmesan cheese
5. Add the sauce to the pasta in the pot and blend.
6. Dehydrate for 6 hours at 145 degrees.
7. To rehydrate, cover with water just above level of food in pot, boil, stir, and serve.

Lasagna

Lazy Lasagna

Serves 4
Weight 1 dried serving = 5 ounces

Quick to assemble, this lasagna features your choice of beef, turkey, or tofu.
1. Heat a large skillet or Dutch oven over medium-low heat. Add:
   1 tablespoon olive oil
   When the oil is hot, add, stirring, for 3 minutes:
   1 onion, minced
   4 cloves garlic, minced
   Add and cook, stirring, 5 minutes longer:
   1 pound ground beef or turkey, or crumbled tofu
2. Reduce heat to low and add:
   5 cups spaghetti sauce
   ¹/₂ teaspoon crushed red pepper flakes
   Simmer for 5 minutes, stirring occasionally.

3. Preheat oven to 350 degrees. Oil a 10-by-13-inch casserole dish.
4. Have ready:
   > **9 sheets of uncooked *oven-ready* lasagna noodles**
5. Finely grate:
   > **8 ounces (1 cup) mozzarella cheese**
   > **8 ounces (1 cup) Parmesan cheese**
6. Layer the ingredients in the casserole dish in the following order:
   > **$^1/_4$ of the sauce, 3 of the sheets of noodles, $^1/_3$ of the grated mozzarella, and $^1/_3$ of the grated Parmesan. Repeat, using all the ingredients and topping the casserole with the last $^1/_4$ of the sauce.**
7. Cover and bake for 30 minutes; then uncover and bake 10 minutes longer. Let stand outside the oven for 10 minutes.
8. Use a spatula to break up the noodles and spread on covered dehydrator trays.
9. Dehydrate for $5^1/_2$ hours at 145 degrees.
10. To rehydrate, cover with water just above level of food in pot, boil, stir, and serve.

Southwestern Lasagna
Serves 4
Weight 1 dried serving = 6.5 ounces

1. Have ready:
   > **1 cup salsa, mild, medium, or hot**
   > **5 cups spaghetti sauce**
   > **9 sheets of uncooked *oven-ready* lasagna noodles**
   > **6 ounces soy ground round, uncooked, or 10 ounces sautéed ground beef**
   > **1 pound ricotta cheese**
2. Preheat oven to 350 degrees. Oil a 10-by-13-inch casserole dish.
3. Finely grate and combine:
   > **8 ounces (1 cup) Monterey Jack cheese**
   > **8 ounces (1 cup) Parmesan cheese**
4. Layer the ingredients in the casserole dish in the following order:
   > **$^1/_4$ of the spaghetti sauce, 3 of the sheets of noodles, $^1/_3$ of the salsa, $^1/_3$ of the ground round, $^1/_3$ of the ricotta, and $^1/_3$ of the grated cheeses. Repeat, using all ingredients and topping the casserole with the last $^1/_4$ of the spaghetti sauce.**

5. Cover and bake for 30 minutes; then uncover and bake 10 minutes longer. Let stand outside the oven for 10 minutes.
6. Use a spatula to break up the noodles and spread on covered dehydrator trays.
7. Dehydrate for 5 hours at 145 degrees.
8. To rehydrate, cover with water just above level of food in pot, boil, stir, and serve.

Summer Lasagna

Serves 4
Weight 1 dried serving = 6 ounces

---

1. Have ready:
   5 cups spaghetti sauce
   9 sheets of uncooked *oven-ready* lasagna noodles
2. Heat a large skillet or Dutch oven over medium heat. Add:
   2 tablespoons olive oil
   When the oil is hot, add and sauté for 3 minutes:
   1 onion, minced
   2 cloves garlic, minced
   Add and sauté 5 minutes longer:
   10 fresh mushrooms, diced
   3 zucchini, diced
   Remove from heat and stir in:
   4 eggs, beaten
   ¹/4 cup dry white wine
   2 tablespoons chopped fresh basil or parsley leaves
   15 ounces canned small white beans, rinsed and drained
3. Preheat oven to 375 degrees. Oil a 10-by-13-inch casserole dish.
4. Finely grate:
   8 ounces (1 cup) Parmesan cheese
5. Layer the ingredients in the casserole dish in the following order:
   ¹/4 of the spaghetti sauce, 3 of the sheets of noodles, ¹/3 of the vegetable mixture, and ¹/3 of the grated cheese. Repeat, using all the ingredients and topping the casserole with the last ¹/4 of the spaghetti sauce.
6. Cover and bake for 30 minutes; then uncover and bake 10 minutes longer. Let stand outside the oven for 10 minutes.
7. Use a spatula to break up the noodles and spread on covered dehydrator trays.

8. Dehydrate for 6 hours at 145 degrees.
9. To rehydrate, cover with water just above level of food in pot, boil, stir, and serve.

Crab Lasagna

Serves 4
Weight 1 dried serving = 7 ounces

---

1. Heat a large skillet or Dutch oven over medium-low heat. Add:
   2 tablespoons olive oil
   When the oil is hot, add, stirring, for 3 minutes:
   1 onion, minced
   2 cloves garlic, minced
   Stir in:
   $^1/_2$ cup whole wheat flour
   $^1/_4$ teaspoon salt
   $^1/_4$ teaspooon cayenne pepper
   Slowly add and cook, stirring until smooth:
   2 cups milk
   Set aside.
2. Preheat oven to 350 degrees. Oil a 10-by-13-inch casserole dish.
3. Have ready:
   1 pound cooked crabmeat or imitation crab, flaked
   9 sheets of uncooked *oven-ready* lasagna noodles
   8 ounces ricotta cheese
   28 ounces canned crushed tomatoes
4. Finely grate:
   8 ounces (1 cup) Parmesan cheese
5. Layer the ingredients in the casserole dish in the following order:
   $^1/_4$ of the onion sauce, $^1/_4$ of the tomatoes, 3 of the sheets of noodles, $^1/_3$ of the crab, $^1/_3$ of the ricotta, and $^1/_3$ of the Parmesan. Repeat, using all the ingredients and topping the casserole with the last $^1/_4$ of the onion sauce and $^1/_4$ of the tomatoes.
6. Cover and bake for 20 minutes; then uncover and bake 10 minutes longer. Let stand outside the oven for 10 minutes.
7. Use a spatula to break up the noodles and spread on covered dehydrator trays.
8. Dehydrate for $5^1/_2$ hours at 145 degrees.
9. To rehydrate, cover with water just above level of food in pot, boil, stir, and serve.

Casseroles

Zucchini Casserole

Serves 4
Weight 1 dried serving = 7 ounces

1. Cook, then drain in a colander:
      2 cups (14 ounces) orzo (barley-shaped) pasta
   Return pasta to the pot and set aside.
2. Heat a heavy skillet over medium-low heat. Add:
      ¼ cup olive oil
   When the oil is hot, add, stirring:
      ½ cup whole wheat flour
   Add slowly, stirring constantly:
      2 cups milk or any variety stock
3. Add the sauce to the pasta in the pot, along with:
      5 zucchini, grated
      1 onion, minced
      4 ounces canned diced green chilies
      1 cup grated cheddar cheese
      ½ cup finely grated Parmesan cheese
      1 teaspoon salt
      ½ teaspoon cayenne pepper
   Stir well.
4. Preheat oven to 350 degrees. Oil a 10-by-13-inch casserole dish.
5. Spread the pasta mixture in the casserole dish. Sprinkle evenly over the top:
      ¼ cup pork or soy bacon bits
      1¼ cups whole-grain bread crumbs
   Dot the casserole with:
      1 tablespoon butter or margarine
   Bake uncovered for 40 minutes.
6. Spread on covered dehydrator trays and dehydrate for 6 hours at 145 degrees.
7. To rehydrate, cover with water just above level of food in pot, boil, stir, and serve.

Tortilla Chip Casserole

Serves 4
Weight 1 dried serving = 7 ounces

1. Bring to a boil in a large saucepan:
   1 cup any variety stock
   $^1/_4$ teaspoon salt
   Add:
   1 zucchini, diced
   1 bell pepper, minced
   1 onion, minced
   3 cloves garlic, minced
   Reduce heat and simmer for 5 minutes, or until just tender.
2. Preheat oven to 350 degrees. Oil a 10-by-13-inch casserole dish.
3. Have ready:
   18 ounces blue corn (or other variety) tortilla chips,
   slightly crushed
   $3^1/_2$ cups spaghetti sauce
   $1^1/_4$ cups grated Monterey Jack cheese
4. Layer the ingredients in the casserole dish in the following order:
   $^1/_3$ of the spaghetti sauce, $^1/_2$ of the chips placed in an
   even layer, $^1/_2$ of the cheese, and $^1/_2$ of the vegetables.
   Repeat, using all of the ingredients and topping the
   casserole with the last $^1/_3$ of the spaghetti sauce.
5. Spread over the casserole:
   $^1/_4$ cup salsa, mild, medium, or hot
   Pour over the casserole:
   $^1/_2$ cup any variety stock
6. Bake, covered, for 25 minutes.
7. Spread on covered dehydrator trays and dehydrate for $5^1/_2$ hours at 145 degrees.
8. To rehydrate, cover with water just above level of food in pot, boil, stir, and serve.

Shrimp-Corn Bake

Serves 4
Weight 1 dried serving = 6.5 ounces

1. Preheat oven to 350 degrees. Oil a 10-by-13-inch casserole dish.
2. Beat together in a large bowl:

> **6 eggs**
> **$1/4$ cup corn oil**
> **two ears fresh corn kernels (about $2^1/2$ cups kernels)**
> **$1/2$ cup finely grated Parmesan cheese**
> **$2^1/2$ cups milk**
> **1 onion, minced**
> **8 ounces uncooked shrimp, shelled, deveined, and diced**
> **$1^1/4$ cups polenta corn meal**
> **$3/4$ cup whole wheat flour**
> **$1/2$ teaspoon baking soda**
> **$1/2$ teaspoon salt**
> **$1/4$ teaspoon cayenne pepper**

3. Pour the shrimp mixture into the casserole dish and bake for 25 minutes, or until toothpick inserted in center comes out clean.
4. Remove from oven and let stand for 10 minutes.
5. Spread on covered dehydrator trays and dehydrate for 5 hours at 145 degrees.
6. To rehydrate, cover with water just above level of food in pot, boil, stir, and serve.

Tuna-Cheese Soufflé Casserole

Serves 4
Weight 1 dried serving = 4.5 ounces

1. Bring to a boil:

> **$1^3/4$ cups water**

Add:

> **$1^1/2$ cups whole wheat couscous**
> **$1/2$ teaspoon salt**

Stir, cook for 15 seconds; then cover, turn off heat, and set aside.
2. Preheat oven to 350 degrees. Oil a 10-by-13-inch casserole dish.

3. Beat together:

    4 eggs
    $^1/_2$ cup mayonnaise
    2 tablespoons fresh lemon, orange, or grapefruit juice
    1 onion, minced
    1 bell pepper, minced
    14 ounces canned water-packed tuna, drained
    $^1/_2$ teaspoon salt
    $^1/_8$ teaspoon cayenne pepper

4. Spread the cooked couscous in the casserole dish. Sprinkle over it:

    $^1/_2$ cup finely grated Parmesan cheese

Spread the tuna mixture over the cheese.

5. Bake for 30 minutes, or until lightly browned.
6. Using a spatula, break up the soufflé and spread on covered dehydrator trays.
7. Dehydrate for $4^1/_2$ hours at 145 degrees.
8. To rehydrate, cover with water just above level of food in pot, boil, stir, and serve.

Cheddar Casserole

Serves 4
Weight 1 dried serving = 3.5 ounces

---

1. Finely chop:

    1 large eggplant, scrubbed but not peeled

Cover it with water in a saucepan. Boil for 5 minutes, then drain in a colander.

2. Preheat oven to 350 degrees. Oil a 10-by-13-inch casserole dish.
3. Spread the eggplant evenly over the bottom of the dish. Spread evenly over the eggplant:

    8 slices whole wheat bread, crumbled
    $^3/_4$ cup grated sharp cheddar cheese

4. Beat together in a large bowl:

    6 eggs
    $2^1/_2$ cups milk
    1 tablespoon cornstarch
    4 cloves garlic, minced
    $^1/_2$ teaspoon salt

$^1/_2$ teaspoon cayenne pepper
$^1/_2$ teaspoon ground nutmeg
1 bunch fresh spinach, finely chopped (3 cups chopped)

5. Pour the milk mixture over the eggplant, bread, and cheese.
6. Bake for 25 minutes or until firm.
7. Spread on covered dehydrator trays and dehydrate for 6 hours at 145 degrees.
8. To rehydrate, cover with water just above level of food in pot, boil, stir, and serve.

Falafel Casserole

Serves 4
Weight 1 dried serving = 6.5 ounces

Falafel mix gives an instant Middle-Eastern flair to a simple dish.

1. Bring to a boil:
     1$^1/_4$ cups water
   Add:
     1 cup whole wheat couscous
     $^1/_2$ teaspoon salt
   Stir and cook for 15 seconds; then cover, turn off heat, and set aside.
2. Beat together in a large bowl:
     6 eggs
     $^1/_2$ cup water
   Add:
     2 cups dried falafel mix
     8 ounces feta cheese, crumbled
3. Preheat oven to 350 degrees. Oil a 10-by-13-inch casserole dish.
4. Spread the cooked couscous in the dish. Spread evenly over it:
     2 cups plain yogurt
   Spread the falafel mixture over the yogurt. Bake for 25 minutes.
5. Break up the casserole with a spatula and spread on covered dehydrator trays.
6. Dehydrate for 4 hours at 145 degrees.
7. To rehydrate, cover with water just above level of food in pot, boil, stir, and serve.

Devil's Gate Crab Casserole

Serves 4
Weight 1 dried serving = 5.5 ounces

This is devilishly easy.

1. Cook, then drain in a colander:
   12 ounces fettucini pasta, broken in thirds
   Return pasta to the pot. Stir in and blend well:
   1 cup mayonnaise
   1 bell pepper, minced
   1 onion, minced
   3 stalks celery, minced
   1 pound cooked crabmeat or imitation crab, flaked
   2 tablespoons hot sauce
   $^1/_2$ teaspoon salt
2. Preheat oven to 350 degrees. Oil a 10-by-13-inch casserole dish.
3. Spread the crab mixture in the dish. Sprinkle evenly over the top:
   2 slices whole-grain bread, crumbled
   Dot with:
   1 tablespoon butter or margarine
4. Bake for 30 minutes.
5. Spread on covered dehydrator trays and dehydrate for 6 hours at 145 degrees.
6. To rehydrate, cover with water just above level of food in pot, boil, stir, and serve.

Blue Cheese Potato Puff

Serves 4
Weight 1 dried serving = 5 ounces

1. Place in a small bowl:
   1 cup TVP (textured vegetable protein)
   Cover with:
   $1^1/_3$ cups boiling water
   Let stand for 5 minutes.
2. Bring to a boil in a large saucepan:
   9 medium baking potatoes (about 4 pounds)
   10 cups water
   Reduce heat and simmer for 30 minutes. Drain the potatoes, peel them, and then mash them in the pot using a potato masher or fork. Set aside.

3. Preheat oven to 350 degrees. Oil a 10-by-13-inch casserole dish.
4. Combine the TVP with the mashed potatoes. Stir in:

> 2 tablespoons butter or margarine
> $1^1/4$ cups (5 ounces) crumbled blue cheese
> 1 bunch spinach, minced (3 cups minced)
> 1 bell pepper, minced
> 1 cup milk
> 8 eggs, beaten
> 1 tablespoon hot sauce
> 1 teaspoon salt

Stir well.
5. Spread the potato mixture in the casserole dish. Bake for 40 minutes, or until puffed and firm.
6. Spread on covered dehydrator trays and dehydrate for $5^1/2$ hours at 145 degrees.
7. To rehydrate, cover with water just above level of food in pot, boil, stir, and serve.

Sweet Potato Casserole

Serves 4
Weight 1 dried serving = 7 ounces

1. Cover with water and bring to a boil in a large saucepan:

> 6 sweet potatoes (about $3^1/4$ pounds), scrubbed but not peeled, ends snipped off

Reduce heat and simmer for 40 minutes, or until fork-tender.
2. Drain the potatoes and mash them in the pot, along with:

> 2 tablespoons butter or margarine
> 1 cup TVP (textured vegetable protein)
> juice of 1 fresh lemon (2 tablespoons juice)
> 8 eggs, beaten
> 1 cup finely grated Parmesan cheese
> $1/2$ teaspoon salt

3. Preheat oven to 350 degrees. Oil a 10-by-13-inch casserole dish.
4. Spread the potato mixture in the dish. Sprinkle over the top:

> 2 cups whole-grain bread crumbs
> $1/2$ cup pecans, finely chopped

Dot with:

> 1 tablespoon butter or margarine

5. Bake for 25 minutes.
6. Spread on covered dehydrator trays and dehydrate for 5 hours at 145 degrees.
7. To rehydrate, cover with water just above level of food in pot, boil, stir, and serve.

Fish Baked with Onions

Serves 4
Weight 1 dried serving = 5.5 ounces

1. Cook, then drain in a colander:
   2 1/2 cups (16 ounces) orzo (barley-shaped) pasta
   Set aside.
2. Heat a large skillet over medium-low heat. Add:
   2 tablespoons olive oil
   When the oil is hot, add and cook for 5 minutes:
   3 onions, minced
   2 cloves garlic, minced
3. Stir in and cook 2 minutes longer:
   6 whole ripe tomatoes, diced (about 5 cups)
   juice of 2 fresh lemons (4 tablespoons juice)
   1 teaspoon salt
   1/2 teaspoon freshly ground black pepper
4. Preheat oven to 350 degrees. Oil a 10-by-13-inch casserole dish.
5. Spread the cooked pasta in the casserole dish. Spread evenly over the pasta:
   1 pound boneless skinless fish fillets (cod, flounder, or sole)
6. Pour the sauce evenly over the fish. Bake for 25 minutes.
7. Spread on covered dehydrator trays, flaking the fish.
8. Dehydrate for 6 hours at 145 degrees.
9. To rehydrate, cover with water just above level of food in pot, boil, stir, and serve.

Summer's Bounty

Serves 4
Weight 1 dried serving = 6.5 ounces

1. Preheat oven to 350 degrees. Oil a 10-by-13-inch casserole dish.
2. Beat together in a large bowl:

   12 eggs
   1/4 cup olive oil
   1 1/2 cups finely grated Parmesan cheese
   1/4 cup minced fresh basil or parsley leaves
   6 cloves garlic, minced
   9 cups minced (bell pepper, onion) or grated (summer
       squash, carrot) vegetables
   7 cups whole-grain bread crumbs
   1 teaspoon salt
   1/2 teaspoon freshly ground black pepper

3. Spread in the casserole dish and bake for 30 minutes or until light brown.
4. Spread on covered dehydrator trays and dehydrate for 6 1/2 hours at 145 degrees.
5. To rehydrate, cover with water just above level of food in pot, boil, stir, and serve.

Gnocchi

Serves 4
Weight 1 dried serving = 5.5 ounces

This is easy to make from semolina or quick-cooking farina flour.

1. Combine in a bowl:

   3 cups milk
   1 1/2 cups semolina (or quick-cooking farina)
   1/2 teaspoon crushed red pepper flakes
   1/2 teaspoon salt

2. Heat in a large heavy saucepan until just boiling:

   2 cups milk

   Slowly add the semolina mixture to the boiling milk, stirring constantly, until thick. Remove from heat.

3. Preheat oven to 350 degrees. Oil a 10-by-13-inch glass casserole dish.

4. Beat in a medium bowl:

> **5 eggs**

Add one cup of the hot mixture to the eggs. Beat well, then return the mixture to the saucepan. Blend thoroughly; then stir in:

> **$^3/_4$ cup finely grated Parmesan cheese**
> **$^3/_4$ cup grated mozzarella cheese**

5. Pour the mixture into the casserole dish. Spread evenly over the top:

> **3 cups spaghetti sauce**

6. Bake for 15 minutes, or until bubbly on top and lightly browned on bottom.
7. Spread on covered dehydrator trays and dehydrate for 6 hours at 145 degrees.
8. To rehydrate, cover with water barely above level of food in pot, boil, stir, and serve.

Other Combination Dishes

Shrimp Jambalaya

Serves 4
Weight 1 dried serving = 4.5 ounces

1. Place in a saucepan:

> **1$^1/_2$ cups quinoa, rinsed and drained**
> **2$^3/_4$ cups water**

Bring to a boil; then reduce heat and simmer for 20 minutes or until tender and translucent. Set aside.

High in protein, the grain quinoa has a nutty flavor and pleasant consistency.

2. Heat a Dutch oven over medium-low heat. Add:
    2 tablespoons olive oil
When the oil is hot, add and stir for 10 minutes:
    1 onion, minced
    1 bell pepper, minced
    10 fresh mushrooms, minced
3. Stir in, bring to a boil, then simmer 5 minutes longer:
    28 ounces canned crushed tomatoes
    15 ounces canned small white beans, drained
    8 ounces uncooked shelled, deveined shrimp, minced
    2 teaspoons minced fresh thyme or 1 teaspoon dried
      thyme
    $^1/_2$ teaspoon salt
    $^1/_4$ teaspoon cayenne pepper
4. Add the quinoa to the shrimp mixture and blend.
5. Spread on covered dehydrator trays and dehydrate for 6 hours at 145 degrees.
6. To rehydrate, cover with water just above level of food in pot, boil, stir, and serve.

Black Bean Stroganoff

Serves 4
Weight 1 dried serving = 6 ounces

1. Bring to a boil in a saucepan:
    $1^1/_2$ cups water
Add:
    $1^1/_4$ cups whole wheat couscous
    $^1/_2$ teaspoon salt
Stir and cook for 15 seconds; then cover, turn off heat, and set aside.
2. Heat a large skillet or Dutch oven over medium-low heat. Add:
    4 tablespoons olive oil
When the oil is hot, add and sauté for 5 minutes:
    2 onions, minced
    6 fresh mushrooms, minced
Reduce heat to low. Add and cook 2 minutes longer:
    $^3/_4$ cup whole wheat flour

Add slowly, stirring, until smooth and thick:
> **2 cups milk**
> **2 cups plain yogurt**
> **15 ounces canned black beans, rinsed and drained**
> **2 teaspoons dry mustard**
> **$1/2$ teaspoon salt**
> **$1/8$ teaspoon cayenne pepper**
> **$1/8$ teaspoon ground nutmeg**

3. Combine cooked couscous and sauce. Stir in:
> **$1/4$ cup white wine**

4. Spread on covered dehydrator trays and dehydrate for 6 hours at 145 degrees.

5. To rehydrate, cover with water $1/2$ inch above level of food in pot, boil, stir, and serve.

Cashew Curry

Serves 4
Weight 1 dried serving = 6 ounces

1. Bring to a boil in a saucepan:
> **$1^2/3$ cups water**

Add:
> **$1^1/3$ cups whole wheat couscous**
> **$1/2$ teaspoon salt**

Stir and cook for 15 seconds; then cover, turn off heat, and set aside.

2. Heat a Dutch oven over medium heat. Add:
> **1 tablespoon canola oil**

When the oil is hot, add and cook for 5 minutes:
> **1 onion, minced**
> **1 pound fresh mushrooms (18 to 20 mushrooms), diced**
> **3 cloves garlic, minced**

3. Stir in and cook for 3 minutes:
> **1 cup finely chopped cashews**
> **1 teaspoon salt**
> **1 teaspoon crushed red pepper flakes**
> **1 teaspoon ground ginger**
> **1 teaspoon ground turmeric**
> **$1/2$ teaspoon ground cumin**
> **$1/2$ teaspoon ground cinnamon**

4. Stir in the couscous and:
    3¹/₂ cups any variety stock
    ¹/₄ cup raisins, chopped
    2 large tomatoes, chopped (2 cups)
    ²/₃ cup TVP (textured vegetable protein)
    Bring to a boil; then reduce heat and simmer for 3 minutes.
5. Spread on covered dehydrator trays and dehydrate for 5 hours at 145 degrees.
6. To rehydrate, cover with water ¹/₂ inch above level of food in pot, boil, stir, and serve.

Vegetable Chow Mein

Serves 4
Weight 1 dried serving = 6 ounces

1. Heat a Dutch oven over medium heat. Add:
    1 tablespoon sesame oil
    When the oil is hot, add a combination of any of these fresh vegetables, in the following order:
    5 cups diced fresh vegetables (onions, carrots, broccoli,
    green beans, eggplant, summer squash, mushrooms,
    bell peppers, or peas)
    Cook and stir for 15 minutes, or until tender.
2. Reduce heat to low and add:
    8 eggs, beaten
    ¹/₂ cup TVP (textured vegetable protein)
    2 tablespoons fresh ginger, minced
    1 tablespoon tamari soy sauce
    1 tablespoon hot sauce
    12 ounces chow mein noodles
    Cook and stir for 5 minutes.
3. Spread on covered dehydrator trays and dehydrate for 4¹/₂ hours at 145 degrees.
4. To rehydrate, cover with water just above level of food in pot, boil, stir, and serve.

Stir-Fried Salmon

Serves 4
Weight 1 dried serving = 5.5 ounces

1. Bring to a boil in a medium saucepan:
   1 1/2 cups quinoa, rinsed and drained
   2 3/4 cups water
   Reduce heat and simmer for 20 minutes, or until tender and translucent. Set aside.
2. Heat a large skillet or Dutch oven over medium-low heat. Add:
   2 tablespoons olive oil
   When the oil is hot, add and stir for 5 minutes:
   1 onion, minced
   2 bell peppers, minced
   3 cloves garlic, minced
   Add and cook, stirring, for 3 minutes:
   1 pound uncooked fresh boneless skinless salmon
   **   steaks, diced**
3. Add:
   28 ounces canned crushed tomatoes
   1/4 cup red wine
   1 fresh jalapeño pepper, seeded and minced
   1/2 teaspoon salt
   1/4 teaspoon freshly ground black pepper
   Cover and cook 5 minutes longer.
4. Mix quinoa with salmon mixture.
5. Spread on covered dehydrator trays and dehydrate for 6 hours at 145 degrees.
6. To rehydrate, cover with water just above level of food in pot, boil, stir, and serve.

Feta Cheese Couscous

Serves 4
Weight 1 dried serving = 5 ounces

1. Bring to a boil:
   2 cups water
   Add:
   1 3/4 cups whole wheat couscous
   1/2 teaspoon salt
   Stir, cook for 15 seconds; then cover, turn off heat, and set aside.

2. Heat a large skillet over medium-low heat. Add:

> **1 tablespoon olive oil**

When the oil is hot, add and cook for 5 minutes:

> **1 onion, minced**
> **2 cloves garlic, minced**
> **1 carrot, grated**

3. Stir in:

> **3 cups spaghetti sauce**
> **one 6¹/₂-ounce jar marinated artichoke hearts plus**
> **liquid, diced**

4. Blend the couscous with the sauce.
5. Spread on covered dehydrator trays and dehydrate for 5 hours at 145 degrees.
6. To rehydrate, cover with water just above level of food in pot, boil, stir, and serve.

Fresh Green Pea Curry

Serves 4
Weight 1 dried serving = 5 ounces

---

1. Heat a Dutch oven over medium-low heat. Add:

> **1 tablespoon olive oil**

When the oil is hot, add:

> **1 onion, minced**
> **2 tablespoons minced fresh ginger**
> **3 cloves garlic, minced**

Cook for 5 minutes, stirring occasionally.

2. Stir in and cook 2 minutes longer:

> **1 carrot, grated**
> **1 teaspoon ground turmeric**
> **¹/₄ teaspoon cayenne pepper**

3. Add and bring to a boil:

> **7 cups any variety stock**
> **1¹/₂ cups dried lentils, rinsed and drained**
> **³/₄ cup whole wheat couscous**

Reduce heat and simmer, covered, for 45 minutes, or until lentils are tender.

4. Stir in and cook 2 minutes longer:

    8 ounces fresh or frozen petite shelled peas
    (about 1 1/2 cups)
    1 teaspoon salt

5. Spread on covered dehydrator trays and dehydrate for 6 hours at 145 degrees.
6. To rehydrate, cover with water 1/2 inch above level of food in pot, boil, stir, and serve.

Crab Frittata

Serves 4
Weight 1 dried serving = 6 ounces

1. Cook, then drain in a colander:

    14 ounces capellini pasta, broken in thirds

    Return pasta to pot and set aside.

2. Whisk together in a large bowl:

    8 eggs
    2/3 cup milk
    3 cloves garlic, minced
    2 teaspoons fresh oregano, minced, or 1 teaspoon dried
    oregano
    1/2 teaspoon salt
    1/2 teaspoon freshly ground black pepper
    1 pound raw or cooked crabmeat or imitation crab, flaked

3. Preheat broiler.
4. Heat a large *ovenproof* skillet over medium-low heat. Add:

    2 tablespoons olive oil

    Swirl the oil to coat bottom of skillet. When the oil is hot, add the egg mixture. Cover, reduce heat to low, and cook for 10 minutes, or until firm on edges and bubbling in center.

5. Uncover the skillet. Sprinkle the frittata with:

    1 cup finely grated fresh Parmesan cheese

6. Place the skillet under the broiler for 5 minutes, or until firm, browned, and puffy.
7. Break up frittata and mix it with the pasta.
8. Spread on covered dehydrator trays and dehydrate for 6 hours at 145 degrees.
9. To rehydrate, cover with water just above level of food in pot, boil, stir, and serve.

Suggested Reading

Bell, Mary. *Mary Bell's Complete Dehydrator Cookbook*. New York: William Morrow & Co., 1994.

Conners, Tim and Christine. *Lipsmackin' Backpackin'*. Helena, MT: ThreeForks Books, 2000.

Costenbader, Carol W. *The Big Book of Preserving the Harvest*. Pownal, VT: Storey Books, 1997.

DeLong, Deanna. *How to Dry Foods, 2nd Edition*. Tucson, AZ: H.P. Books, 1992.

Furness, Bruce W., M.D., Michael J. Beach, Ph.D., Jacquelin M. Roberts. "Giardiasis Surveillance—U.S., 1992–1997," *Centers for Disease Control MMWR Surveillance Summaries*. August 11, 2000.

Kesselheim, Alan S. *Trail Food: Drying and Cooking Food for Backpacking and Paddling*, Rev. Ed. Camden, ME: Ragged Mountain Press, 1998.

Miller, Dorcas S. *Backcountry Cooking*. Seattle, WA: The Mountaineers, 1998.

Morris, Michele J. "Stoves," *Backpacker*. March 2002.

———. "Water Treatment,"———.

Ried, Adam. "Can an Oven Thermometer Make You a Better Baker?" *Cook's Illustrated*. March/April 2002

United States Department of Agriculture Food Safety and Inspection Service. "Focus on: Sausages," June 1995.

University of California, Berkeley. "Ask the Experts," *UC Berkeley Wellness Letter*. March 2002.

White, Joanna. *The Dehydrator Cookbook*, Rev. Ed. San Leandro, CA: Bristol Publishing Ent., 1998.

Yaffe, Linda Frederick. *High Trail Cookery: All-Natural, Home-Dried, Palate-Pleasing Meals for the Backpacker*, Rev. Ed. Chicago: Chicago Review Press, 1997.

———. *The Well-Organized Camper*, ———, 1999.

INDEX